The Campus And The People

Organization, Support and
Control of Higher Education
in the United States
in the Nineteen Sixties

by
M. M. Chambers

Copyright, 1960
by
M. M. Chambers

Library of Congress Catalog
Card Number
60-16964

Available from:
THE INTERSTATE
Printers & Publishers, Inc.
Danville, Illinois

Author's Preface

/

THE CAMPUS AND THE PEOPLE represents one man's observations and reflections about education beyond the high school in the United States. Ten separate essays, all first published in periodicals between April 1959 and June 1960, have been revised here and there and put together. Though not initially organized in this sequence, the thoughts expressed have a certain coherence and consistency, I trust, and form something of a recognizable pattern. They deal almost exclusively with matters of policy relating to the organization of higher education and the support and control of universities and colleges.

Editors and publishers of eight journals in which all these chapters recently appeared have generously granted me permission to adapt and reproduce them in this form. Acknowledgments are due to:

The Michigan Alumnus,
The Michigan Alumnus Quarterly Review,
The Journal of Higher Education,
The North Central Association Quarterly,
The Educational Forum,
College and University Business,
The American School Board Journal, and
School and Society.

Much of the inspiration—a great deal of the stimulus which caused these thoughts to take form—came from many friends and colleagues at the Center for the Study of Higher Education at the University of Michigan, where I have enjoyed pleasant associations during the past two years. First among these is Dr. Algo D. Henderson, Director of the Center and Professor of Higher Education, an educational statesman of the first rank. To him, and to each of my congenial associates of the faculty, administration and staff of the University, and especially to the postdoctoral Michigan Fellows in College Administration and the advanced graduate students who frequent the Center, my gratitude goes.

Ann Arbor, October 1, 1960   M. M. Chambers

M. M. Chambers is a member of the faculty of the Center for the Study of Higher Education, The University of Michigan. The Center is supported in part by funds granted by Carnegie Corporation of New York. The statements made and views expressed in this publication are, however, solely the responsibility of the author.

The Campus
And The People

I

The Few
Or The Many?

Shall we educate the best brains, or shall we provide facilities so that larger and larger numbers have opportunity to progress as far as their aptitudes and ambitions allow? We shall unquestionably do both. This is the mission of higher education in our day.

Many mature men and women now living have personally witnessed and marveled at the advent of the horseless carriage, watched its evolution through the model T and the V-8, and seen the automobile industry become the employer directly or indirectly of one out of every seven persons who work.

These people also remember Marconi and his wireless telegraph. They saw radio receivers come into everyman's home and hotel room, to be followed by the ubiquitous television set; saw two-way radio become commonplace equipment of aircraft, patrol cars and taxicabs; saw radar and sonar enable man's senses to probe the heavens and the waters farther than ever thought possible.

Within a single lifetime the flying machine of sticks and wires and muslin came into being and was metamorphosed into all-metal airplanes and thence to the jet-propelled giants of today, with atomic-powered aircraft just over the horizon. Only yesterday an atomic submarine crossed the top of the world under the polar ice-cap.

The man who can dispatch a thousand huge bombers half-way around the world in a single strike dwarfs the awesome Thor of Scandinavian legend who hurled the thunderbolts; but these weapons

This chapter is adapted from an article first published under the same title in the *Michigan Alumnus* 65 (No. 16): 265-269 (April 11, 1959).

are already obsolescent in the age of intercontinental ballistic missiles, of orbiting sputniks, of interplanetary rockets.

Life Will Never Be the Same Again

There are men among us who have seen and heard the terrifying spectacle of the 'shrieking bugles, thundering hooves, and swinging sabers of the cavalry charge—only to see the automatic small arms, motorized transport, and armored vehicles banish the horse from the world's armies, while sputtering tractors eliminated animal power from America's farms.

Equally swift and spectacular advances in industrial production, medicine and public health, housing and sanitation, continually come. The span of life expectancy has been extended twenty years in our time. If we reflect that all these achievements are in great part due to the patient work of many persons in the shops, laboratories, clinics, libraries and classrooms of colleges and universities, we gain a glimmering of how intimately higher education is related to our humane development, to our individual and national well-being, to our industrial and military might.

As we advance in all these sectors, the conditions of living are changed, the organization of society becomes more complex, and insistent new obligations are thrust upon our institutions. Most of the young persons now in colleges, universities, and graduate schools will see the dawn of the twenty-first century. Those now in high schools can live in the *Anno Domini* 2,000 before they reach the age of sixty. It is only four short decades away. What manner of plan, organization and scope of higher education shall we have for the next momentous decade?

A Mounting Population: A Growing Economy

The Michigan Council of State College Presidents began to study the situation several years ago. In 1954 the Council published a notable little volume on *Future School and College Enrollments in Michigan: 1955 to 1970*. Jointly prepared by three professors—Ronald Freedman of the University of Michigan, Albert Mayer of Wayne, and John F. Thaden of Michigan State, the booklet presented five sets of projections ranging from high to low, based on different conditions assumed.

(2)

Its most optimistic "Projection E" predicts 113,000 students for the fall of 1960 while the actual number of students in Michigan's colleges and universities this year is about 140,000. There is good reason to suppose that the same curve as extended to the year 1970 will continue. The boys and girls who will be of college age in 1969 are now eight years old. There is not much guesswork as to what their numbers will be. They are already on the elementary school rolls. Michigan's college enrollment in 1970 is anticipated to be well over 200,000 students.

In 1955 a second significant pamplet, *The Michigan Economy to 1970: A Study in Growth*, was published by the Michigan Council of State College Presidents. This was prepared by Professors Paul W. McCracken, Richard Lindholm, and Lawrence H. Seltzer. From studies of various trends that had already been charted for twenty-five to fifty years in the past, the authors concluded that by 1970 Michigan may very well have a population of nine million, receiving total income payments of twenty-four billion dollars. This level of income would be seventy-five per cent above that of 1953.

In looking ahead for the next decade, we shall have to envision higher education in Michigan for twice as many young people, in a state having a substantially larger population and an enlarged gross product over today's figures.

Roughly, Michigan has a little less than one-twentieth of the nation's population, and a bit more than one-twentieth of the gross national income. Though not "average," Michigan is not extremely atypical. In such states as California, Arizona, and Florida, for example, the rate of population growth is so great, both presently and prospectively, as to indicate that by 1970 they will have three times as many college students as they have now.

Advancing Technology Upgrades Jobs

But the increase in population and wealth means more than the figures indicate. We have known for a long time that with advancing technology, all jobs are upgraded. The place of the untrained, unskilled, unschooled worker becomes smaller, while the demand for persons at all higher levels of knowledge and skill expands. All jobs move upward —*all jobs*, from those of the research scientist and the design engineer, to that of the least skilled laborer or technician.

Everybody knows we shall need more engineers and scientists and teachers and physicians than we have today. The requirements will not merely increase; they will be compounded.

What is less widely recognized is that the more and more complex organization of industry, business and the professions and public services will not only maintain a voracious demand for top-ranking people as it does even today, but that it also calls insistently and increasingly for unprecedented numbers of middle-rank semi-professional workers and technicians to make up the teams which are essential to the optimum use of top-level talent.

The physician and surgeon work in conjunction with anesthetists, registered nurses, medical technicians, physiotherapists, optometrists, podiatrists, dietitians, laboratory technicians, practical nurses, medical clerks, hospital administrators, pharmacists, medical secretaries and hospital orderlies, to mention a few of the associated occupations at random.

Much of the valuable time of dentists is saved by the work of the dental prosthetist, the dental hygienist, and the dental secretary. The fully professional engineer is assisted, either directly or remotely, by draftsmen, junior engineers, technicians of different types and grades, as well as foremen, time-and-motion-study men, and clerical workers in various capacities. All these are well below the top levels of the profession, but far above the stratum of skilled labor in the ordinary sense.

Upgraded Jobs Require Higher Education

Thus it is that the manufacturers who once maintained or contributed to the support of vocational schools of high-school level, are now calling for, contributing to, and in some cases supporting technical schools of junior college level, four-year schools of technology, five-year schools of engineering, and advanced graduate work in engineering sciences.

Higher education has been largely reorganized and reconstructed within a lifetime to keep pace with advancing technology and the growing complexity of society and high organization of the economy. One can recall when college was for a small handful (4 per cent of the college-age population in the year 1900), whose intelligence and good family and social position enabled them to aspire to one of a few prestige professions, chiefly law, medicine, and theology. There were scarcely any other occupations that were thought to require any education beyond the elementary or common school.

The college preparation for the few professions required a full four years or more (though some gained admission to practice by other means until comparatively recent years), and any student who could not finish the full course was a cast-off, a failure, a misfit. Higher education was a long, narrow ladder with no honorable exit except at the top. It fitted the concept of a tiny "elite corps" who had the benefit of university education, among great masses of "common people" who were thought to be not fit for higher education, or even secondary schooling; not to need it; and foolish to aspire to it. This is no longer the picture of American society.

The idea is European in origin, and foreign to the genius of America. Higher education here is not a strait groove for a tiny few, but a broad-based fountain-head with many outlets at different levels. To be sure, we must identify and provide the best of opportunities for the superior few, so far as that is possible. That is why a suitable plan for Michigan contemplates at least one great university concentrating on advanced graduate and professional instruction and the highest reaches of research, and limiting its undergraduate enrollment by selection. Its graduate levels are for the topmost rank of professional people and researchers.

The Best? Yes, and Many Others, Too

But we must educate not only the best brains. We must also bring the others up to their optimum competencies. The second best, and the third best, until we arrive at least half-way down the scale, are capable of deriving great benefit for themselves and for the national security and welfare from education for middle-rank occupations, semi-professions, and medium-grade technical specialties. Not only that: the educational ladder must be kept ready for those who have the ability to progress upward. Time and again a junior-college graduate in draftsmanship works as a technician for a few years, attends evening classes in an urban university and eventually emerges with a degree in engineering.

Time and again a teacher who first got a normal school diploma eventually has upgraded himself to the bachelor's, master's, and doctoral levels, and into a school superintendency or a college professorship. Even the boy who flunks out in Freshman year sometimes later earns a degree in some other institution; and even if he does not, he is a better man for having had a semester in college than he would have been with no college experience at all.

To perform its function in today's complex and moving society, higher education must be thought of as "education beyond the high school" ranging in duration from six weeks to eight years, with its product going out into myriads of occupations. The problem of admissions is not merely that of screening out all but the most gifted five per cent who show most promise of mastering the lengthiest and most difficult professional education. It is something much more complex and demanding than that. It is scarcely less than assaying the abilities and aptitudes of every applicant; and of seeing that he has his chance to be admitted to some course of study from which he can gain benefit for himself and for the public, in some institution somewhere.

More than a decade ago the President's Commission on Higher Education, after studying the test records of millions of young men in the armed services in World War II, and equating them with the tests most widely used for college admission, concluded that about one-third of the population had the requisite ability to complete four years of college work with success, and that about half of all boys and girls possessed the necessary intelligence to do two years of college work. Persons who ignore these findings are having difficulty with their own superiority-complexes.

Supremely significant as the Commission's conclusions are, they do not provide the whole answer regarding higher education's responsibility today. True enough, a part of the job is to sift and identify the applicants who show indications of success in two years or four years of college. Another part, also of tremendous import, is to provide courses that will stimulate the ambitions and challenge the best effort of the highly talented, the moderately talented, the less talented, and even of those whose talents are less than average.

Our economy needs them all, with their abilities developed to the highest point possible, even if it be only the point attained after a six-weeks' course in some simple form of service.

A Statewide System

It is not to be supposed that any one institution can undertake all this responsibility. The implication is that there will be a diversified system of many institutions of different types. This explains in part why Michigan has sixteen community-junior colleges, with others in the offing; why we have nine state colleges and universities, with four branch institutions in various stages of development. It is one of the reasons why we have some 41 private colleges in Michigan, and why we continue to have in urban centers a considerable number of proprietary technical and commercial schools offering courses as short as six weeks, along with others of six months or one year or more in duration.

It is logical that a great university thrusting up the apex of a broad-based state system, would concentrate much effort on advanced graduate and professional studies and research work, and accordingly it is not surprising, but much too little known, that four out of every ten students at the University of Michigan are above the level of the bachelor's degree.

What of the other six? Three are at senior college stage (third and fourth years), and three are at junior college stage. The University is top-heavy with advanced students, as indeed it should be as the state's principal center of advanced graduate and professional studies. It also presents the unusual spectacle of an undergraduate enrollment which is not bulged at the bottom with large numbers of first and second-year students who will drop by the wayside.

Of course transfers from junior colleges and other four-year institutions help to keep the senior college enrollment in balance; but the fact that these transfers have been screened at other places helps in some degree to save the University from the task of processing hordes of students of whom many would become academic casualties. The primary factor, of course, is the University's wisely selective admissions policies and practices.

Picture, then, Michigan's state system of higher education as a broad-based pyramid. Standing in the center, and running from base to apex of the pyramid, is the enrollment of The University of Michigan, bounded by straight vertical parallel lines (not bulged at the bottom). Grouped around it, and varying in height, sturdiness and contour, are the graphic representations of the enrollments of eight other state institutions, fifteen community-junior colleges, and 41 private colleges.

Each of these has its own particular merits, and each serves, either because of its location or of its character, or both, in ways which no other institution could duplicate.

A junior college, even if a majority of its students are enrolled only one year or less, and even if few ever transfer to other institutions, can be a *good* junior college for its local purposes and for its own clientele, and can be worth much more than its cost to the district and to the state.

The young people who get a year or two of technical and general education beyond high school, and the citizens of the locality who look upon it with some pride as the capstone of the local school system and as a community cultural center, are getting their money's worth. The state and the nation are getting additions to their strength and security. Who shall say that its students, though many of them may have only modest achievements to their credit, should have been denied the college opportunity?

Shall we educate the best brains, or shall we provide facilities so that larger and larger numbers have opportunity to progress as far as their aptitudes and ambitions allow? We shall unquestionably do both. This is the mission of higher education in our day.

Fifty States Make a Nation

Not all states are like Michigan; in fact, not any two are alike; but certain principles and broad policies are applicable in any state, no matter how different its problems may be in detail.

Shall we charge high fees to students who are able to pay? This reactionary concept of selling education under private contract for what the market will bear was never in the minds of the founders of the state universities. The great state universities of the midwest and west were conceived as the summit of the state-wide public school system, free of tuition.

Can the state afford to provide public higher education for large numbers either free or at very low fees? Where is the money coming from? This policy will bring strength to the state's economy which will more than recoup the cost. The educated citizen is a better producer and a better consumer. The states can construct more equitable and more productive revenue systems than any state now has, without harming industry. They can also notice that if state expenditures for higher education were doubled, they would still be a comparatively small dollar drain upon state funds. The average percentage of all state revenues spent for higher education fell from 10 per cent in 1915 to 4 per cent in 1950. It will probably have to go upward to where it was in 1915.

A little redressing of balance in state expenditures is necessary, and a constant refurbishing of state revenue systems must go on. These things are occurring, and will continue.

II

Old Siwash And
The Monster Universities

In the graduate school, the professor's function is to push outward the boundaries of knowledge. He should be qualified to do this by his own investigations and writings, and to coach and inspire and lead his graduate students to develop these same abilities in themselves. Few persons today need to be persuaded that this activity is at the root of progress in all fields of human endeavor.

The prototype of the Alma Mater over which generations of alumni have waxed sentimental is a small college with a few hundred students, all undergraduates. Some hundreds of such colleges continue to dot the landscape, and many of them are gems in the diadem of higher education in America.

Within the most recent half-century the huge universities have grown to a magnitude of from twenty thousand to fifty thousand students each. Far from being a small, homogeneous, close-knit academic community, such an institution is actually in itself a city of considerable size. Besides its liberal arts college and its graduate school, it includes from a dozen to fifteen or more discrete professional and vocational schools whose courses run from a few weeks (as in the winter short courses in the college of agriculture) to seven or ten years or more (as in medicine and law).

Clustered around and between the principal schools of the university is a congeries of research institutes, special study centers, service bureaus, and the like, whose numbers are more or less constantly changing. The mere housing of students involves the operation of dormitory and dining-hall systems which rival big-city hotels in size, to say nothing of hundreds of fraternity and sorority houses, numerous clubhouses of various kinds, and myriads of rooms and apartments in private premises.

Some Consequences of Diversity

At the big universities, doctor's, master's, and professional degrees run far into the hundreds each year, and the baccalaureate is awarded annually to thousands. Commencement ceremonies can be held only in vast football stadiums, and the thousands of graduates must race past the president in quick-step in order to receive their diplomas before the fall of darkness.

Such externals as these give rise to talk of the "monster universities" and to alarmed questionings such as "How large can a university become?" Should we halt the growth of these leviathans and nurture our Old Siwashes? Actually no such choice is necessary, or likely to be. Private philanthropy, which keeps Old Siwash afloat and swimming upstream, is increasing. The state helps by granting tax exemptions and other favors, and the national government encourages gifts by individuals and corporations through generous provisions for deductions in the income-tax and estate-tax laws, only recently made more liberal. If vast fortunes come into individual hands less often than formerly, corporations which dominate the industrial and commercial scene increasingly recognize their obligation to higher education, and their opportunity to gain and maintain good will through substantial contributions to colleges.

Alumni do not confine themselves to sentimental well-wishing alone, but increasingly come through with annual cash contributions, recognizing their moral indebtedness to the college which educated them at less than cost. This habit, once widely established, constitutes what is aptly called a "living endowment," substantially equivalent to a productive investment of many millions. For a quick example, think of two thousand alumni giving annually an average of $20 apiece as the equivalent of one million dollars conservatively invested. Ten thousand alumni giving an average of $40 make the equivalent of an endowment of ten million dollars.

Besides, a college is a valued part of its own community, and can cultivate annual support from that source. In many cases it is also the child of a nationwide or regional church organization which contributes part of its costs of operation. So Old Siwash, particularly if it does its job well and is also ably managed from a fiscal standpoint, goes on

(10)

forever, serving its constituency and providing the distinctive atmosphere and tone, be they denominational or other, which please its clientele. When we sing of "the land of the free" and "sweet land of liberty," the freedoms which we celebrate include the right to operate a reputable private college, to teach in one, to be a student in one, and to contribute financial aid to one or more of our own choice.

We are not sufficiently familiar, however, with the multiple and highly significant differences between Old Siwash and the large universities. Old Siwash is a four-year undergraduate institution, steeped in the liberal tradition. Although it may and often does have fledgling departments of education, home economics, business administration, or studies related to other professions, and although it may have a number of sequences labeled pre-medicine, pre-law, pre-engineering, and so forth, it does not offer the advanced professional courses nor the advanced specialized work in arts and sciences that is to be found only in a university graduate school.

Even in the most populous and wealthiest states and cities, there can as yet be only a few centers where these advanced professional and graduate studies can be provided on a high-quality basis. This fact alone accounts in large part for the emergence of the "monster universities."

Universities Nourish Graduate Schools

The large universities are rapidly moving toward a point where a major fraction of their students will be at the graduate level. To name but a single example, currently at the University of Michigan four out of ten students are above the bachelor's level, working in the Horace H. Rackham School of Graduate Studies or in the advanced professional schools. This is a fact much too little known, and one which has important financial implications, as we shall soon note.

Why do not the big universities drop their undergraduates and become strictly graduate schools, in the European tradition? As much as a century ago this thought was favored by Tappan of Michigan, later by Gilman of Hopkins, Jordan of Stanford, and Harper of Chicago—all giants in their day—but never succeeded. The reasons are many. American high schools have never emulated the German *gymnasien*, the French *lycées*, or the English "public schools," all of which are elite secondary schools of six or more years, carrying their students to about the level of our fourteenth grade, or midway in our undergraduate college. College admission is naturally based upon high-school

(11)

graduation, and thus our freshmen and sophomores are somewhat immature and unprepared by European standards. Many of our state universities and land-grant colleges were at first required by statute to admit all high-school graduates resident in the state, regardless of other qualifications, and some are still under that compulsion. Moreover, today several of the professional courses bridge the line between undergraduate and graduate levels, and should not be truncated by being placed partly in one institution and partly in another.

Of course relief is already in progress to prevent the large universities from having their seams burst by increasing masses of first-year and second-year students. Several of the largest and most renowned state universities—notably California and Michigan—have highly selective admissions practices, and reject applicants who do not seem to have good chances of succeeding in college. Many states (among which California, Texas, Washington, Minnesota, Michigan, Illinois, and Florida are good examples) have extensive networks of local public two-year colleges attended by local youth who can not afford to travel away from home or who find it difficult to be admitted to a four-year college for any reason.

This community-junior college is the most rapidly growing segment in American education. Evidence from many states indicates that graduates of its "college-parallel" courses are able to transfer to four-year colleges and universities and continue with success. At the same time graduates of its vocational, technical, or other courses not intended as a basis for further formal schooling are better prepared for work and citizenship than they would otherwise be; and many adults in its community derive much benefit from its formal courses and informal cultural activities designed for them.

One can commend this development unreservedly, and urge its expansion; but it will never wholly relieve the "monster universities" of first- and second-year students, nor will it ever usurp or infringe upon the functions of Old Siwash. In every community there will always be a few students who will have the means and the desire to go directly from high school to a large university, and, assuming that their intellectual and other qualifications justify it, the opportunity to plunge immediately into the stimulating atmosphere of a world-renowned intellectual center should not be denied to them. It may pay large dividends to them and to their nation.

There will also always be some students who will prefer to go from high school to a small liberal arts college of their choice—an Old Siwash, if you will—where they can get four years, or maybe two or three years, of life in close association with a small faculty under the elms of a quiet village where just the right religious atmosphere prevails or just the preferred ethical tone is maintained. For many eighteen- or nineteen-year-olds, not yet ready for the stiff competition and more impersonal attitudes of a larger place, or perhaps not intending in any event to have more than four years in college, this choice may be superb.

The Shapes of the Graphs Are Changing

In fact the spread of the community-junior college will quickly be found to be a buttress for Old Siwash. Nearly all colleges are now troubled financially and otherwise by the fact that a graph of their enrollment is bulged at the bottom: that is, they have comparatively large freshman and sophomore classes filled with students who will soon fail or transfer to other institutions, leaving only slim quotas in the junior and senior classes. In small colleges this means that a great deal of the upper division instruction must be in needlessly small classes, which makes it inordinately expensive, because of less than full use of faculty talents, building space, and costly instructional equipment.

As soon as these small colleges receive transfers from two-year community-junior colleges, the effect is manifest. Skimpy enrollments in the upper division are beefed-up and in time the graph may bulge at the top, or at least approach the contours of a perpendicular straight-sided column. The immediate financial gains from this situation are hardly more noteworthy than the numerous other advantages sure to accrue from the increased maturity and competency of the student body as a whole. Indeed, it is not at all unlikely that this development may eventually justify some four-year colleges in adding a fifth year and offering the master's degree in some departments, where the preponderance of advanced students would enable them to do so efficiently and at no great added expense.

In short, a network of community-junior colleges can bring opportunity for higher education to thousands to whom it would otherwise be denied. The four-year and five-year colleges will survive and thrive as never before. The "monster universities" will continue to be large universities, and continue to have many undergraduate students, but will increasingly become graduate and advanced professional institutions. Their graphs will bulge at the top. Now we are ready to consider some financial implications. Costs of instruction vary with the level of the instruction. They also vary with size of class, amount of costly equipment required, and other factors.

There Are Fiscal Implications

What would you think if you were told that in a given year a four-year college with an enrollment of 1,300 students spent for educational and general purposes $750 per student, and that in the same year a large university in the same state, having an enrollment of 24,000 students, spent $1,300 per student? I hope you would want to ask some questions before giving your answer.

Did the large university include 800 medical students whose instruction costs $3,000 to $4,000 a year? Does its medical school have post-graduate departments and medical research institutes which few medical schools maintain? Does it also have a dental school, a school of public health, a school of veterinary medicine? How many students are in its law school, its engineering schools, and each of its other professional schools? Does it operate a school of music? A school of fine arts and architecture? How many students in each of these schools are above the bachelor's level? How many students are in the graduate school of arts and sciences? How many doctoral degrees are granted per year? How many master's degrees? Other specialized degrees?

The state of Texas, in devising a formula representing the cost of teachers' salaries (the principal element in the cost of instruction) at different levels, distinguishes eleven types of instruction and then slices these horizontally, one stratum representing undergraduate instruction as a whole, one instruction at the master's level, and one at the doctoral level. For the liberal arts (excluding sciences) the ratio is roughly 1 to 2 to 6½. For engineering it is approximately 1 to 3 to 6, with the costs at each level about 50 per cent higher than for the liberal arts. Medicine is so much higher that it is not included in the formula at all.

In a complex system of colleges and universities, something like the Texas cross-hatching is desirable. First distinguish the several types of curriculums (mainly according to professional schools) and then dissect four strata: (1) junior college, (2) upper division, (3) master's level, and (4) doctoral level.

Economic Consequences

It is at the doctoral level that costs are and ought to be most widely out of line (save perhaps in medical instruction), and most difficult to predict and standardize. This is the "growing edge" of human knowledge. This is where advanced students and professors in equal numbers often participate alike in lengthy seminars; where five professors spend portions of their working time with one advanced student; where the space, equipment, technical and clerical assistance and other essential expenses for individual research projects may be quite considerable. The stakes are high, and the risks are also great. Some doctoral candidates, after substantial expenditure of time and money by themselves and by the university, fail to earn the degree. Some of the research reports, though accepted as a basis for awarding the degree, apparently are of trivial consequence. But here also is the point where revolutionary discoveries are sometimes made, and where the great discoverers of the future are trained.

It may be that Thomas Edison and Henry Ford never went to college; but no one thinks that the technological geniuses of tomorrow will be trained in news-butchering or bicycle repairing. They will come from the graduate schools—perhaps via the industrial laboratories—but certainly from the graduate schools.

And likewise the discoverers in medicine, in the social sciences, the humanities, the arts, philosophy, and in every field that challenges the human mind.

The time has already arrived when the extent and quality of the research facilities and the research and professional leadership afforded by the presence of a large university are of inestimably greater significance in attracting and holding productive industries in a state or region than any petty considerations such as comparative personal or corporate income-tax rates. Preoccupation with beating down income taxes would in the end be suicidal for the industries as well as the state.

Education at any level from kindergarten upward has constructive economic consequences. The higher the level, the larger the results become. We must recognize that the "monster universities" are not merely vast aggregations of football-crazy undergraduates, living a carefree country-club life of ease for four years at the expense of their parents and the taxpayers, while thick-spectacled professors strive vainly to inspire them with a zest for learning. In fact, the big universities have some of the best students from all corners of the world, undergraduate as well as graduate. More and more they are becoming in large part advanced graduate schools.

No state has more than a handful of these, and at least half a dozen states of smaller population have none. With few exceptions the more renowned graduate schools are in the larger universities. Here is a level of learning much more divergent from that of the four-year undergraduate college than the latter is from that of the high school.

The large universities are unrivaled centers of intellectual stimulation not only for hundreds of thousands of students, but also for whole states and regions. They are unsurpassed levers of progress. Costs of instruction in their graduate and advanced professional schools are not fairly to be compared with Old Siwash. The types and levels are not comparable.

The university consists chiefly of many things that Old Siwash never was and never hopes to be; and Old Siwash itself is something that the university does not pretend to be. Diversity is the glory of our educational system.

The Upper Higher Learning

In this country, "education beyond the high school" is synonymous with "higher education."

We do not reflect often enough that this makes of higher education a highly diversified enterprise which may be of any duration from a few weeks of technical training to nine or ten years of university study. You may be inclined to sniff and say six weeks in a technical school for a post-high-schooler is not higher education, but let's not argue that too strenuously. We have long been accustomed to thinking of higher education as four years in college—the undergraduate years leading to the bachelor's degree. Until relatively recent years practically all students in even the larger universities were undergraduates. A "college education" meant a four-year period of study, not unmixed with a little football and maybe a bit of horseplay.

In the wholesome stereotype of many decades, on a June day in his senior year, the college student stepped up with his mortarboard at an awkward angle and received the parchment proclaiming him a bachelor of something or other, heard the R.O.T.C. bugler sound the "call to the work of the world," and his college days were over.

The picture has gradually changed. There are now well over a third of a million students in the graduate schools of American universities. This is more students than were in all the colleges and universities at the beginning of this century. More than sixty-five thousand master's degrees are conferred every year by six hundred institutions. Each year approximately nine thousand men and women don the three velvet chevrons and the flowing multicolored hood of the doctorate, not counting doctors of medicine, dentistry, and veterinary medicine.

A hundred and eighty institutions offer the doctor's degree, and over a hundred of them confer it upon as many as half a dozen candidates each year. About sixty universities each turn out forty or more new doctors annually. Forty-one universities are members of the Association of American Universities, an organization more than half a century old which is a starchy clique of institutions having "select" or prestigious graduate schools, and which includes most of the larger ones. About thirty universities produce a hundred or more doctors each per year, and about fifteen turn out two hundred or more each. Some twenty-five graduate schools award sixty per cent of all doctorates.

The Peaks Above the Timber Line

Great universities are no longer four-year institutions; they are seven-year or eight-year composites. The graduate school is at the head of the column, on top of the heap, the apex of the pyramid. Many students of medicine, law, theology, and, to lesser extent, some other professions are also in this somewhat rarefied level above that of the bachelor's degree. It is well to observe that some of the universities are *not* pyramids, with great numbers of freshmen and sophomores always constituting a broad base. Instead, a graphic representation of the student population in a given year will resemble a perpendicular column. There are as many students in the fifth and sixth years as in the first and second; and the third and fourth years are also as populous as the first. This is because a university attracts transfer students from many other types of institutions into its upper division and graduate courses. In fact, this tendency is so strong that the better universities are beginning to "bulge at the top." At the University of Michigan, as already noted, four students out of ten are above the bachelor's level.

These students are for the most part in the graduate school of arts and sciences; but hundreds of them are in medicine, dentistry, law, social work, education, public administration, and the upper stages of engineering, business administration, pharmacy, and various other professional curriculums. The University at Ann Arbor has more graduate students than all other institutions in the state combined—though the total enrollment at the University, including undergraduates, is only perhaps one-sixth of the combined college enrollments in the state.

(17)

There are sixty-two colleges and universities (including seventeen junior colleges) in the state, but only three of them offer doctoral degrees. Only about a dozen offer master's degrees, and in nearly half of these this is on an almost negligible scale. Institutions having graduate instruction on a substantial scale ought to be sharply differentiated in the public mind from the more numerous undergraduate colleges—not for any reason of snobbishness, or of size, or of anything but the valid reasons why we distinguish "college" from "high school" and "graduate school" from "college."

We must learn to think of colleges and universities in carefully discriminating terms. Even if we temporarily disregard all questions of size and quality, they vary greatly as to the *level* of instruction.

Why Is Graduate Education Different?

First, the graduate school provides opportunity for a deeper specialization. Second, the graduate school requires more independence. The student chooses his own subjects and his own papers, and defends them in person against expert criticism, in the company of his peers. Third, and most important, the graduate school provides for and requires investigation and research on the frontiers of knowledge. This means not only seminar rooms, libraries, laboratories, shops, clinics and observatories. It means also investigation and field observation in industrial plants, hospitals, school systems, commercial establishments, farms, villages, government offices, and a vast variety of public and private social agencies.

No standard college library will suffice. There must be available *all* the up-to-date literature of a thousand specialties. Laboratories and shops cannot be of the high-school or college variety. The advanced graduate student must often have rare and costly materials, unique and expensive equipment, and ample space in which to conduct his scientific trials in his particular specialty. His instruction must often be in small seminars or in individual conferences with one or more professors who are giants in their fields—themselves great researchers, writers, discoverers, not merely amiable and patient pedagogues.

For the doctoral degree, after demonstrating his mastery of at least a reading knowledge of two foreign languages, and passing a stiff comprehensive examination over the broad field in which his specialization lies, the candidate is usually placed under the tutelage of a committee of five senior professors who will advise him at various stages of his research undertaking, and against whose penetrating criticism he must defend his final dissertation. In the graduate school, the professor's function is to push outward the boundaries of knowledge. He should be qualified to do this by his own investigations and writings, and to coach and inspire and lead his graduate students to develop these same abilities in themselves. Few persons today need to be persuaded that this activity is at the root of progress in all fields of human endeavor.

Some activities of this kind go on, of course, in industrial research laboratories and in scientific establishments operated by the national government. Some go on in almost every national and state governmental department which is well conducted under superior leadership. Some go on in many social, charitable, and penal agencies. Some go on at agricultural experiment stations, and in armed forces hospitals, proving-grounds, and missile ranges. Some go on in pastors' studies, in far-flung mission stations, and in the international cooperation activities of various kinds carried on by the United Nations and by the United States and other national governments.

This ceaseless penetrating of the peripheries of knowledge is not a monopoly of the graduate schools; but wherever it goes on in significant fashion, it will usually be found that the men and women who are its spearheads had their apprenticeship in the graduate schools. The universities cannot and do not claim to be the sole centers for the advancement of knowledge and wisdom; but they are the training-grounds from which emerges an endless and increasing stream of reinforcements for the forces of enlightenment in the perpetual war against ignorance. Their influence is literally worldwide. Theirs is the endless frontier.

Nothing Risked, Nothing Gained

Graduate study is costly. The professors must be the best in their fields. Other universities and private industries are constantly competing for their services, which are bid for in a nationwide or international market. Much of the work with students is done individually, face to face. Advanced graduate students are not taught in masses. The essential laboratory equipment, fieldwork facilities, and library facilities are always expensive, and sometimes fantastically so. Moreover, the enterprise is not routinized and channeled over familiar ground so that the destination is predictable with any certainty. Each research project is a stab in the dark, a risky trial, an unpredictable long-shot. Often it is built upon only an intuitive hunch which may pay off enormously or which may prove to be a total failure. If the investigator knew in advance what his findings would be, there would be no point in undertaking the research.

These are among the reasons why the cost of operating a graduate school may be anywhere from twice to ten times as high per student as the cost of operating an undergraduate college. This explains why universities having substantial graduate schools should be set off in a distinct category when we think of higher education.

For the sake of the freedoms of individual choice which we prize, it is necessary that the undergraduate colleges should be of many types and sizes, espouse a variety of aims and methods, and foster diversity in organization and goals. These results are favored by the existence of a large number of private colleges, all of which traditionally have almost complete freedom to manage their own academic and fiscal affairs. Among the state colleges not having substantial graduate schools (many of them former normal schools and teachers' colleges) there is perhaps a greater degree of sameness. All must eschew any denominational dominance; almost all are located regionally within the state for the purpose of making more or less similar opportunities available to youth in all parts of the state. If they offer a year of graduate study it is only in a few departments, and their efforts in the graduate field are limited and rudimentary, not in any broad sense comparable to university graduate schools. They are much more numerous than the universities, and their existence in a state system of higher education has much to do with two recent tendencies in state government: (1) the extension of control by non-educational state fiscal and administrative officers over institutions of higher education, and (2) the creation of statewide educational boards to govern or coordinate all the state's colleges and universities as one unified system.

It may be that as the volume of the public higher educational enterprise increases, devices bearing some similarity to the foregoing may become unavoidable for public institutions at the undergraduate level. In fact, these devices are now in use on a more widely prevalent scale than is generally realized. The crucial question is whether they can properly be extended to include the universities and the graduate schools, where freedom and diversity are of the essence, and where advancing the peaks of excellence takes primacy over large-scale work of a somewhat routinized nature.

Can graduate study be operated on a "formula" basis, with costs per semester-hour held within narrow limits, with the ratio of professors to students required to be at a figure similar to that in the lower schools, with costs of apparatus and equipment rigidly channeled according to undergraduate standards, and with teachers' salaries on an inflexible and narrow scale? An inexorable downgrading would inevitably follow. From the viewpoint of the public interest, it is better to build one pinnacle of topmost quality than merely to perpetuate mass mediocrity. In graduate study and research, no state can afford to blunt the point of its spear.

III

Diversify The Colleges

Somehow we must blueprint, if at first but dimly, the shape of a system of higher education fit for a rapidly expanding college population in the seventh and eighth decades of the twentieth century. Higher education in America must be pluralistic, not monolithic. We must not bar the doors by raising fees to prohibitive levels or by establishing rigidly selective entrance examinations throughout the system. That would repudiate the American tradition of varied opportunity, and would reduce the oncoming stream of educated manpower—in itself a calamity.

Varied types of institutions, decentralized forms of control, and diverse educational philosophies have long been characteristic of higher education in the United States. This is a hallmark of strength and a harbinger of growth. Since the founding of the first state universities in the last decade of the eighteenth century, we have had a dual system embracing public and private colleges. The state institutions have always been outnumbered by the private colleges, and during most of the nineteenth century they were also generally outstripped in prestige; but today they enroll well over a majority of our students, and some of them are as renowned as any centers of learning in the world.

A ferment in the 1850's led to the establishment of a few "farmers' colleges" and culminated in the enactment by Congress of the famed Morrill land-grant act of 1862, which, with a long train of subsequent supplementary acts, encouraged a new type of higher education on a nation-wide scale. Every state and territory now has at least one land-

This chapter was first published under the same title in the *Journal of Higher Education* 31: 9-13 (January 1960).

grant institution (sixteen states have two). To this innovation, with its emphasis on the applied sciences in agriculture and engineering, we now recognize that we owe much of the nation's tremendous productivity on farms and in factories.

Within the last decade we have begun to export this spectacularly fruitful type of higher education. As everyone knows, many a team of teachers and specialists in research and extension programs, temporarily on leave from an American land-grant university, is today at work in some underdeveloped country on the other side of the globe, endeavoring to help transplant the means of diffusing among a large and impoverished population the know-how which can transmute the local resources into higher standards of human welfare. In short, we seek to assist those countries in diversifying their programs of higher education.

Among state institutions, variations are many, and their range is wide. It has come about that in somewhat more than half of our states, the state university and the land-grant college are one and the same. Among these institutions are California, Illinois, Minnesota, Ohio State, and Wisconsin. In about a score of other states the land-grant institution is separate, located at a distance from the state university, and not under its administrative control (though in a few instances both institutions, and sometimes others, are under one governing board). Several of these separate land-grant establishments have made phenomenal progress in size, scope, and quality, and are now large cosmopolitan universities, in fact if not in name. Indeed, their names have undergone an evolution, often lagging somewhat behind their actual development. First designated as "state college of agriculture and mechanical arts," an institution often later became "state college," and finally "state university." In some instances this results in a somewhat confusing nomenclature, as in Michigan, where the historic state university is the University of Michigan at Ann Arbor and the land-grant institution at East Lansing has recently been named Michigan State University.

In the sparsely populated Mountain States of the Far West, as well as in a few of the small northeastern states, most of the state institutions are comparatively small; this is especially true where there are several state institutions of different types, as in Montana and New Mexico. So the gamut runs from small to large, and the institutions vary in a hundred other ways that would require much space to catalogue. But this is not half the story. Some forty states have a total of over 160 degree-granting state institutions, originally established as "normal schools," which evolved into four-year "state teachers colleges"; often subsequently into "state colleges" with cognate curriculums in arts and sciences and occasionally in home economics, commerce, or engineering; and eventually, in a few instances, into "state universities" with authority to confer graduate degrees. (Witness the two in Ohio: Bowling Green State University and Kent State University.)

Only a fractional part of the existing diversity has been hinted at. In smaller numbers of states there are separate state schools of mines, state schools of forestry, state colleges for women, state colleges exclusively or largely for Negroes (some land-grant and some other), state military colleges of high standing, and an occasional state technological college (non-land grant). We have said nothing of state junior colleges. The picture is one of vast variety: in programs of offerings, in admission requirements and practices, in characteristics of the student bodies, in numbers enrolled, in costs of attendance, in quality of faculties and instruction, in prestige value, and in many other aspects. This is a fortunate circumstance.

Freedom of Choice and Breadth of Opportunity

Colleges and universities under private control are more diverse than public institutions and at least twice as numerous, but in recent years they have enrolled somewhat less than half of all students. In this large group are many nonsectarian institutions (that is, institutions operated by non-profit corporations having no denominational ties) and a great many more church-related ones whose charters provide for some connection with a specific religious body. The Roman Catholic colleges and universities constitute a substantial and widely distributed group; there are some Jewish institutions; and nearly every one of the Protestant denominations maintains a "board of education" which exercises some oversight in respect to a group of several institutions whose operation is connected, sometimes rather tenuously, with the denomination. Here it should be mentioned that these church-related colleges, when incorporated for nonprofit educational purposes—as virtually all of them are—have repeatedly and consistently been held by the courts to be corporations subject to the state laws relating to educational corporations and not to the laws touching religious associations. Thus they are not, by virtue of their character as artificial persons, entitled per se to the particular favors or subject to the special disabilities which the law places upon religious societies; nor are they legally amenable to any external control by the sponsoring denomination except such as may be unmistakably stipulated in their respective charters.

(25)

Each of many groups of private institutions has its own traditions, its own standards, and its own methods, perhaps rather similar to, but never identical with, those of any other; and, of course, there are substantial variations within groups. Some of the old, nonsectarian universities are among the wealthiest institutions in the world from the standpoint of endowment funds; many of the small Protestant colleges struggle continually and valiantly but never seem to obtain as much financial support as they need or as many students as they could accommodate. Indeed, the history of nearly every state records the dissolution of many private colleges, some of which served their purposes well and had creditable careers in their day.

The comparatively small, private, liberal-arts college is the type which has been regarded, during a large part of our history from colonial days onward, as the nucleus and backbone of American higher education. So secure is its place in the sentiments of the public in general that it will undoubtedly continue for a long time to play a key role. But can it be that that role is coming to be shared to some extent by the community junior colleges on the one hand, and, on the other, by larger institutions in which advanced vocational and professional instruction is suitably blended with strong strands of general education?

However that may be, the tradition of freedom and diversity is priceless. A thousand colleges, each formulating its own purposes and standards, and achieving its particular merits in its own way, make for freedom of choice and breadth of opportunity. This is especially true when our systems of accreditation (largely voluntary) and our modern modification of what used to be rigidly required prerequisite sequences make it possible for students to transfer from one institution to another without prohibitive loss of time or money.

It is tempting to dwell on the past and expatiate at length on the elements of variety in the present scene—but our problems lie in the future. Somehow we must blueprint, if at first but dimly, the shape of a system of higher education fit for a rapidly expanding college population in the seventh and eighth decades of the twentieth century.

Main Features of the Blueprint Are Clear

Higher education in America must be pluralistic, not monolithic. We know that in the decade of the 1960's, college enrollments will climb swiftly, and we shall soon have nearly twice as many students as we have ever had before. We must not bar the doors by raising fees to prohibitive levels or by establishing rigidly selective entrance examinations throughout the system. That would repudiate the American tradition of varied opportunity, and would reduce the oncoming stream of educated manpower—in itself a calamity. To be sure, the privately controlled institutions can voluntarily make their admission requirements as difficult as they choose, and it may be hoped that some of them will make the hurdles high. Moreover, at least the leading state university in each of the more populous states might very well be allowed to adopt the policy of admitting only superior applicants to several of its colleges and schools, as it already does in the case of its college of medicine. This would tend to keep the university atmosphere charged with the ozone of high intellectual effort and to maintain the tone of a place in which excellence is prized. This would increase the quality of diversity in the state-wide system of higher education, and would permit the principal state university to control its own growth so as not to swell to the proportions of an educational leviathan.

There are many who believe that the danger of succumbing to mass mediocrity is real if, with a growing college population, our universities and colleges become huge and overcrowded. When this view is taken, the answer must be that we shall have more colleges. The logic of events has already produced this answer. We have some six hundred junior colleges—many privately controlled and many public. Some of the latter are branches of state universities or are separate state institutions, and others are capstones of local public-school systems. Some of the private junior colleges serve chiefly their immediate localities, whereas others draw their clienteles from large regions or from the nation as a whole. The general tendency is for junior colleges to serve the youth who live within commuting distance, and also to assume the functions of a center of adult education and cultural extension for the community; and thus they are coming to be spoken of aptly as community colleges.

Some of these, located in populous and growing localities not over-supplied with educational facilities, have already become four-year, degree-granting colleges, and no doubt this may occur in additional places in the future; but it is clear that the two-year local junior college has a function of enormous importance—to provide the first two years of education beyond the high school for the swiftly increasing numbers of competent high-school graduates in the home community, some of whom would be barred from higher education by financial inability if the junior college were not at hand, and the rest of whom would flock to the state university and other four-year institutions, overcrowding them in the first two years.

Long experience in California and other states shows that the local public junior college can give more than satisfactory preparation for further higher education, and that it can also offer suitably varied, terminal, two-year courses for students who will not go further. These can include vocational and technical instruction suited to the wants of industry in the locality, in addition to liberal and general education designed as immediate preparation for good citizenship in the workaday world rather than for advanced university studies.

If more than half of the students in senior college (upper two years) in California and Mississippi are graduates of local junior colleges, does this not indicate that the community junior college can relieve the state universities and the other four-year institutions of some of the prospective flood of students in the first two years, and at the same time produce for them an increased inflow of well-prepared senior-college and graduate students? These are among the numerous advantages of the development of additional community junior colleges as a significant part of our increasingly diversified American system of higher education.

IV

Something Could Be Added
To the Self-Surveys

There are in every county-seat town perhaps 25 to 50 key persons in various public agencies and in various private organizations who can collectively furnish a mountain of extremely interesting data regarding the place and the people: the current panorama, the pageant of the past, and a good deal of what is in store for the future. These key people are generally affable, good-humored, genuinely interested in their work, and willing to talk about it and give out written materials when requested by representatives of a nearby college who obviously want the information for none other than constructive purposes.

The idea of the institutional self-investigation has undoubtedly served long and well as a means of discovering new paths of service for great universities as well as an instrument for the upgrading of non-accredited colleges. In fact, the device is so widely accepted and so much respected that several universities, among which are some state-controlled and some private, have long since established at a high level in their administrative structure an "office of institutional research" which is literally a continuous self-study. The talent engaged in the leadership of these enterprises is generally of a very high order.

It would be difficult to offer a penetrating critique of what is being done in the whole area. It would be presumptuous to attempt it without long and concentrated investigation. Let us confine our focus to the comparatively small college or community-junior college, such as those within the territory of the North Central Association of Colleges and

This chapter was first published under the same title in the *North Central Association Quarterly* 33: 281-284 (April 1959).

Secondary Schools, of which many have recently completed self-surveys or may be considering or definitely planning such undertakings.

The Institution's Setting

The available guides for such enterprises usually suggest that the clientele of the institution be studied, often in connection with its purposes —which is indeed an apposite juxtaposition. But in none of the recent college and junior college self-survey reports which have appeared, has there seemed to be an adequate and really enlightening treatment of what may be called the demographic setting of the institution, and of its anthropographic and economic backdrop. In simpler words, there is seldom if ever to be found any reasonably comprehensive traverse of the socio-economic and geopolitical characteristics of the district or region principally served by the college, projected in depth and developed with cognizance of past changes, current trends, and probable future tendencies.

Two-year and four-year colleges have already become largely local institutions essentially, with relatively few exceptions. This is too well known to require documentation. Some of the exceptions are a few well-endowed private colleges, chiefly in the northeastern states, which are purposely operated as national boarding-schools, selecting their students from many states, and having no intent to serve their immediate vicinages, other than incidentally and on a negligible scale. There are also many denominational colleges and junior colleges, operated primarily as boarding-schools and drawing students largely from the membership of their own respective church organizations, often from many states as well as many foreign countries. These latter institutions, however, are often hospitable to at least limited numbers of students from the immediate locality, and usually do not entirely exclude local applicants on sectarian grounds alone.

For the purely boarding-school type of college, it may perhaps be said that there is no geographically compact constituency; therefore studies of the area within a radius of 50 miles or of 75 miles might be of little more than casual interest. The main considerations are a pleasant spot for the campus and satisfactory avenues of transportation and communication to and fro between it and the outside world. Of course other considerations may sometimes enter. A great medical college of national repute was once said to be so located in a large city that a strong patrol of armed guards had to be posted around the women's dormitory nightly to prevent invasion by hoodlums from the streets.

These exceptions aside, the fact remains that a majority of small colleges are and will become increasingly agencies for the service primarily of the people of an area within a radius of 50 or 75 miles or so from their campuses. Of course nearly all of them may continue to maintain residence halls and have a minority of their students from distant places; and this is certainly advantageous from the viewpoint of outgrowing provincialism among the student body. But if half of the students live within the circled locale, or if this is likely to be true in the future, then an ambitious survey of that district would seem to be an indispensable element in the institution's self-study.

Many Sources of Information

From the United States Bureau of the Census and other divisions of the Department of Commerce information applicable specifically to the counties within the area, regarding their agricultural products and their respective rankings as income-producers, and similar data concerning manufacturing industries, transportation enterprises and commercial establishments can be readily obtained, to say nothing of population data including distribution by sex and age-groups, occupations, and other characteristics. Additional data regarding large and small business enterprises can be gleaned from such standard sources as Dun and Bradstreet's, and from local chambers of commerce or the state chamber of commerce or a similar organization in a nearby large city. Often the state departments of commerce or of labor and industrial relations can furnish pertinent information.

From the state department of public instruction data will be readily forthcoming as to the pupil-population of the public elementary and high schools of the region. The diocesan headquarters will have statistics of Roman Catholic parochial schools. The state department of health will have the statistics of births and deaths, and will be able to estimate with great accuracy the numbers of persons of college age who will be living in the area ten years or fifteen years from now, leaving out of account the probable effects of out-migration and in-migration, which will have to be estimated by other means.

Local county offices of the agricultural extension service and of the soil conservation service will be able to tell much about the character and productivity of the soils, the situation as to flood-prevention, reforestation, drainage, and irrigation. Data of these kinds not available locally can often be had from state or national sources, even including detailed aerial photographs of all or selected parts of the region, as well as soil-maps of individual farms. From the state Farm Bureau Federation, state Grange, or state unit of the Farmers' Union data as to the membership, officers, and activities of local branches of these farm organizations can be had. Similar information regarding labor organizations can be obtained. County offices of the state employment service always have up-to-date statistics and labor-market information. County welfare offices can tell how many persons are receiving public assistance in various categories and what sums are spent annually for those purposes. The county superintendent of schools can exhibit a map of all public school districts in the county, besides giving an earful of school problems and of plans for the future of the public schools.

In fact, there are in every county-seat town perhaps 25 to 50 key persons in various public agencies and in various private organizations who can collectively furnish a mountain of extremely interesting data regarding the place and the people: the current panorama, the pageant of the past, and a good deal of what is in store for the future. These key people are generally affable, good-humored, genuinely interested in their work, and willing to talk about it and give out written materials when requested by representatives of a nearby college who obviously want the information for none other than constructive purposes. Many of them, of course, are themselves college graduates, and feel a certain bond with other college people. They are usually easy to interview. From such contacts the local or nearby college stands to gain much more than merely the information first asked for. It gains friends —influential friends—who will continue to have a certain curiosity about its progress and a particular interest in its welfare because they have given it a little help, however small.

Local Social Field Studies

There are limitations to the data which can be had locally, or even from state and national agencies. After these sources have been exhausted, small local field surveys can be made. The state university, or maybe some other large university nearby probably has a bureau of business research, an institute of public administration, a department of rural economics and sociology, a school of social work, and an institute of social surveys. All of these are interested in the type of thing here discussed. They can probably furnish some data out of hand, and upon request they will usually give advice and expert consultation, and even actual personal assistance, in planning and executing local surveys. They have young instructors and advanced graduate students who, under the guidance of seasoned professors, are actually looking for opportunities to be of just such service. Not to be overlooked in this listing are the university bureaus of educational research and of school service, and departments of adult and continuation education. Some universities maintain a committee on college relations whose function is to cooperate in all feasible ways with other colleges in the state or region. Some universities now have departments of higher education which, in addition to teaching advanced graduate students and conducting and directing research, are always ready to advise and consult with other colleges regarding local problems.

It is of great importance that a college should know as much as possible about the situation and prospects of the young people of its locality. How long do they stay in the lower schools, and why do they leave? Aside from the more obvious cases, why do some of the high-school graduates go to college, while others of equal ability do not? Do many of the youth want a type of education the college does not offer? Where do they go and what do they do after graduation from high school? After graduation from junior college or college? How many leave the community altogether? What jobs are they in and what remuneration do they get? What do the local industries estimate will be their requirements for numbers of employees, and at what levels of training, next year, five years ahead, and ten years ahead? What of the morale of today's young people? Are their attitudes apparently good? What do they want most? Can the abler half of them be brought in as good permanent partners in the college enterprise?

Some of the answers to these questions must be sought by organized and purposeful personal contacts with the boys and girls and young men and young women. Such an enterprise is a youth survey. A small manual on the subject is cited below.[1] It is out of print, but is available in many libraries, including college libraries. If a college faculty, especially the staffs of the several departments in the social science division, and individuals in any other departments who have a real interest in the work, will organize and execute some research of the

---

[1] Chambers, M. M., and Howard M. Bell. *How to Make a Community Youth Survey*. Washington: American Youth Commission of the American Council on Education, 1938. Pp. 50. Not now on sale, but available in many libraries.

types briefly suggested in the foregoing paragraphs, enlisting the aid of some of their ablest advanced students and of some of the alert professional and business persons in their college town, it will be found to be an eminently satisfying and productive undertaking. Besides it is an essential prelude to the more strictly introspective type of institutional self-study which is often difficult to initiate without incurring some faculty suspicion and hostility, not to say truculence or obduracy.

Starting with the great outdoors beyond the ivied walls, in the community of ordinary earthy persons who go about their daily concerns with an engaging matter-of-factness, an overly-introspective college faculty can find that a social survey is a matter-of-fact affair which can and usually does produce invaluable results. Then they are the more ready to apply the same or similar techniques to the internal affairs of their own institution. They are the more able to envision it as a living, growing organism, fitting itself to changed conditions in its environment, as all organisms must. Such, I take it, is one of the aims of a self-survey.

V

The Signposts
Sometimes Shift

Here are my views. What are yours? Let us compare, contrast, and criticize. What is the weight of the evidence? Can we develop some techniques of investigation or experimentation that may produce new facts and new insights for all of us?

The essence of learning and of teaching is the pursuit of truth. Conscientious learners and teachers espouse this ideal with an almost religious fervor, as well they may; for the occupation of either student or teacher seems peculiarly hollow and meaningless unless it consists of the search for what is true.

In the heyday of the German universities, much was made of *Lehrfreiheit und Lernfreiheit* (teaching-freedom and learning-freedom); and indeed the concept has had some vitality in universities everywhere from their beginnings. There have been many times and places where it has been pushed into temporary eclipse; but it is hardly disputable that to the extent to which an institution lacks scholarly freedom for students and teachers, it is not a university, but only a propaganda-mill.

Academic freedom leads to disputation because truth does not appear to all men alike. Reasonable, tolerant, and courteous exposition of clashing arguments is an excellent intellectual exercise, well calculated to facilitate the clarification and diffusion of truth. But precisely because the striving for verity is so intimately a part of man's emotional drives, it easily arouses passions which may override courtesy, tolerance, and cool reason. It may then substitute prejudices of emotional origin for

This chapter was first published under the same title in the *Educational Forum* 23: 447-452 (May 1959).

the fruits of intellectual effort, and pass on to various stages of obstinacy and truculence. Thus one man's truth becomes another man's anathema; and in his passion for truth as he sees it, the one man wants to silence the other.

Thus through all human history, he who would voice his views of truth without reserve has often met with opposition, obloquy, persecution, or even martyrdom. Often the hated concepts have been universally accepted as authentic scientific discoveries a generation or a century later, and their first proponent subsequently enshrined as an intellectual giant and benefactor of the race. Unfortunately this can not be retroactive, but it can perhaps be of some help in the continuing search for truth in the future.

Practical Limits Exist

It is possible that one man's truth, if acted upon, may be, to all his compatriots, treason. Under American concepts of civil rights, a treasonable thought is not a crime, but a seditious utterance may be, and a treasonable action assuredly is. Thus freedom of speech, even as all the freedoms protected by the Amendments to the United States Constitution, has its practical limits. Defining those limits in specific cases is a delicate and continuing task of the federal courts. But each citizen, too, must individually determine those practical limits for himself as he charts his own course in accord with his own conscience and with his own estimates of what is wise and expedient in his own time and place.

I do not say he must be guided exclusively by his own conception of truth at the time, and throw aside all considerations of expediency or caution. That choice is for him alone. I do say that his own view of truth may change somewhat with the years; and that at any time, early or late in his career, a certain quality called by some such name as scientific caution or intellectual reserve will prevent him from being too brazenly sure of the rightness of his own views. He may present them enthusiastically and persuasively, but not dogmatically.

Thus it may be said with a good deal of cogency that the more intelligent a man's devotion to truth, the less likely is he to encounter what seem to him to be odious restrictions of his academic freedom. If he is nevertheless impelled to propound aggressively views which arouse unfavorable emotional reactions in a great majority of his contemporaries, or which clash directly with the prevailing *mores*, or strongly antagonize many who occupy positions of leadership and power in the society of his day, he must do so at the risk of some emotional and perhaps illogical or irrational opposition. To the extent that he awakens this sort of antagonism, he will for the time being at least, have created heat rather than light.

Law, Morals, Taste Help Mark the Boundaries

The happy and productive exercise of academic freedom appears generally to be guided by some four considerations. The first is a thoughtful man's decent reluctance to assume his own infallibility in intellectual matters, and his wary self-restraint in declining to adopt a viewpoint except when the evidence in its support seems conclusive.

Another is an appropriate regard for what is the law of the land appertaining to civil rights, and to educational administration. For this purpose it is not sufficient to memorize the pertinent parts of the federal and state constitutions; the law may change somewhat with each new relevant decision of the Supreme Court, and the general climate of civil rights fluctuates widely as decades and generations pass. And civil rights and academic freedom are not identical, though they may be coming closer together.

A third is the bounds of good morals. Few would suppose that profanity or obscenity is protected by freedom of speech; or that the use of slanderous utterance, provocative of retaliation even with physical violence, is acceptable except under the rarest of circumstances. The obligation to be fair and intellectually honest is also a moral one. Morality is distinctly different from observance of law, for many a moral obligation is not enforceable at law.

A fourth consideration consists in the precepts of good taste. We shall not argue whether these rank above or below moral principles, or whether they are of the same order; but they have subtle and far-reaching influence in human relations, and have their place in the progressive refinement of human nature.

Freedom of Inquiry for Student and Teacher Alike

Closely related to the scientific caution or intellectual reserve which restrains one from "going off the deep end" in dogma, is a respect for the intellectual integrity of others which prevents aggressive and unqualified proselyting: "Here is my view, ready-cut for your acceptance. There is no alternative. I have seen the light; all who do not agree with me are in darkness." At least when dealing with students who are at or approaching intellectual maturity, a supreme requisite is to grant the student his own freedom of inquiry: "Here are my views. What are yours? Let us compare, contrast, and criticize. What is the weight of the evidence? Can we develop some techniques of investigation or experimentation which may produce new facts and new insights for all of us?"

To what extent this attitude can properly be maintained in the teaching of immature children, I do not profess to know; but I suspect that it has a rather large place, and also that it can be over-done. Likewise, I suppose it has its limitations in the case of mature students who are of distinctly inferior intellectual caliber. But the competent university student must be his own judge of the evidence in all cases. After this has been granted, the student-teacher relationship is on a candid and potentially productive basis.

Civil Rights and Academic Freedom Are Not Quite the Same

It is also well for students and teachers alike to know and remember that one may be excluded from an educational institution because of an offense which is not of itself contrary to law. In other words, it has long been understood that an institution may maintain within itself a climate of behavior, a "tone," which is more exacting than the norms sustained by the general law of the jurisdiction. Thus students may be denied the privilege of associating themselves with national fraternities, required to live in dormitories, or compelled to take military training, or to submit to medical examinations, to mention only a few recent instances. In earlier years students and faculty were sometimes required to attend daily chapel exercises, and dismissed if they did not.

In this place I shall not expatiate, as I might, upon the numerous court decisions in many states which have sustained the right of a college or university to maintain yardsticks of behavior as well as of scholarship in accord with its own standards. The bill of rights in the federal or state constitution may protect a type of behavior from being treated as unlawful, but no bill of rights as yet compels an educational institution to retain a student or a teacher who violates its reasonable rules. It is true that in relatively recent years an institutional rule or even a state statute excluding students from a state university or college solely on account of their race and color has come to constitute a violation of the Fourteenth Amendment. And although the great restraints of that Amendment apply only to the states and their agencies, and not to privately controlled institutions, New York has had since 1935 a state statute forbidding nonsectarian tax-exempt educational institutions from discrimination on grounds of race, color, or religion. In 1948 the prohibition of racial discrimination was broadened to apply also to denominational institutions. This is but proof that both law and morals are progressive; that what was a century ago largely unthought of, gradually gained wider acceptance as a moral obligation, and is now a subject of legal compulsion.

Good Taste and Academic Freedom

Probably the essence of good taste in human relations consists in consideration for the convictions and feelings of others. One may think a certain belief of his colleague or neighbor is quite erroneous, that it is based on groundless prejudice, that its tendency is harmful to society; yet it is entitled to a modicum of respect as long as it is obviously held with sincerity by a respectable human being. It is no proper target for sarcasm or ridicule, or cause for violent polemics. These are perhaps better reserved for the long outmoded misconceptions of earlier generations; and even in that case the barbs are better directed at the *idea* than at the person. Indeed, use of the *argumentum ad rem* and abstention from the *argumentum ad hominem* deserves to rank in its own right as a major mark of good taste.

There is no purpose of making a long homily on good taste at this point. The subject is mentioned only because what become bitter controversies concerning academic freedom sometimes originate merely in actions which are plainly in atrociously bad taste. For example, in a church-related college affiliated with one particular denomination, as most of them are, is it in good taste for a student or teacher to overtly avow his disbelief in the tenets of that sect, or to deprecate its discipline and all its works? Is it in good taste for him to proselyte aggressively among his colleagues for atheism, agnosticism, or for any religious system or organization markedly different from that to which his institution is connected? As a practical matter, if he does any of these things he may soon be asked to take his talents elsewhere. Can he then say he has been denied academic freedom? The foregoing is not to create a wrong impression that church-related colleges do not tolerate teachers and students of varied religious beliefs or of none; for many of them do so. But most such colleges have highly-prized traditions and a carefully developed atmosphere which it is folly for one or a group of individuals to attempt to destroy or radically alter in the name of academic freedom.

Similar considerations apply under many differing circumstances in our diversified system of higher education. State universities and colleges have been charged with sacrificing academic freedom for political advantage, and private institutions have been accused of shushing free expression in deference to the predilections of wealthy donors or prospective donors, and it has been said that the governing boards of all types of institutions tend to be heavily overweighted with bankers, financiers, and elderly men of wealth whose economic views are generally decidedly those of yesteryear, and who sometimes tend to regard any differing views with strong suspicion and sharp hostility. Good taste as well as good sense will indicate that in such situations a bull-in-the-china-shop approach in the social sciences, careless of offense to the views of others, may arouse antagonisms disruptive of the calm atmosphere of the academic grove. Irrational antagonisms may, indeed, be impossible to avoid; and the foregoing is not intended as a craven counsel of cringing caution which would make teaching an empty exercise. Rather it is a plea for the taste and skill by which the clear light of learning can be kept ablaze and free from the acrid smoke of prejudiced squabbling. Not always, but often, the more heated a controversy grows, the smaller the original point at issue appears, until sometimes it is lost from sight altogether while the quarrel rages on.

The Role of Semantics and of Skill in Communication

In all controversial areas of knowledge, words and phrases have a way of being picked up and used as slogans or labels by one faction or another, and thus acquiring a derivative meaning markedly different from their generic sense, so that flaunting them in the faces of an opposing faction has much the same effect as passing the toreador's cape in front of a fighting bull. Now delicate mastery of language is undoubtedly one of the key aims of all education, though language is only a tool of expression. It is unworthy of university teachers and students to fall into slovenly habits of speaking in clichés, slogans, and platitudes. Using these worn stereotypes in speech is somewhat like brandishing a club in the face of a person who holds differing views, so that the probability of engaging his open-minded attention or of moving him by intellectual persuasion is practically nil.

"Free enterprise system" wears a halo meaning for a majority of Americans. It is all sweetness and light. But a disgruntled minority will tell you it means "freedom of exploitation" and "freedom to starve" for the unemployed. "Private capitalism" is less highly charged emotionally, but your banker would rather you used the gaudier term. "The profit system" has horns and cloven hooves. To many it seems to be an expression both inaccurate and offensive. To a certain minority it is a sharp rapier with which to goad those who are complacent with the economic *status quo*.

All of the three quoted phrases could probably serve about equally well as designations of the current American economic system, were it not that each has become something of a motto or a bludgeon. We shall never solve any problems of economic progress by bandying such terms back and forth. It is better to recognize that our system, though superb in many ways, has multiple imperfections; that it is being and has been constantly modified and rectified on scores of fronts; that it is by no means all black or all white; that no intellectual purpose is served by using "private capitalism" and "state socialism" as emotion-charged epithets, but that each of these terms could be a useful tool if completely shorn of its load of emotional barnacles.

Similar examples abound. Can one expect to be heard with respect and tolerance when he essays a complex and delicate problem, if he uses words that actually resemble the primitive warrior's club more than the modern surgeon's scalpel?

In the preceding paragraphs, does it seem that academic freedom may be strangled between the lines of guideposts marked scientific caution, law, morals, taste, and semantic skill? Is your temperament such that you must mount the barricades and risk martyrdom? I would not dissuade you. But mark the words of the great liberal Justice Benjamin N. Cardozo, who said: "One who is a martyr to a principle—which may turn out in the end to be a delusion or an error—does not prove by his martyrdom that he has kept within the law."

Some prefer more orderly progress to the cataclysmic episode. Jefferson, lost as he was in his admiration of the French, said in effect that we needed a revolution every twenty years. In the one and three-quarters centuries since his prime, our governmental system has lived and grown and progressed without upset. During the same period, the French bid fair to have been governed by five different republics, to say nothing of five monarchies. Compare the merits of evolutionary development with those of radical change.

VI

Freedom for State Universities:
Campus and Capitol

The principal universities in Michigan, Minnesota, California, and several other states are fortunate in the respect that their state constitutions give the university governing boards full control, and protect them from outside meddling in their internal affairs by noneducational administrative functionaries. First established in Michigan more than a century ago, this principle is gaining ground.

For more than 40 years the movement toward centralization of administrative and fiscal control in state governments has gone on. No doubt it has reduced somewhat the overlappings and incongruities that occur in a large and loosely-knit organization, but it has also brought its own quota of excesses and absurdities.

Modern administrative theory now recognizes that the major divisions of a vast and varied service must have a degree of autonomy in the performance of their functions and in the planning of policies within their spheres of responsibility.

Economy and efficiency are not well served if some distant and uncomprehending central office must review and approve too many of the minute details of institutional management. If budget making must be wholly reduced to formula, if every expenditure must receive an off-campus pre-audit, and if all purchases of supplies, all hirings of non-academic employees, and contracts for building and repairs must first trickle through the tortuous channels of a central state bureaucracy, the result is apoplexy at the center and paralysis at the point of action.

Part of this chapter was first published under the same title in *College and University Business* 27 (No. 3): 25 (September 1959).

Most state universities are already large enough to handle all these necessary phases of fiscal management within their own administrative organization. Budget making is peculiarly the province of the president, for budgeting and planning are virtually one and the same. Actually it is a year-round process, spearheaded by some high-level staff member, utilizing the skill and advice of every dean and department head on the campus, and finally approved by the governing board of the institution.

University business offices conduct their own continuous pre-audit of disbursements. Any outside pre-audit is superfluous, productive of duplication, delay, confusion, rigidity and needless irritation. This is not to argue against a thorough annual *post*-audit of university finances by an authority outside the institution and unconnected with it. Universally recognized is the desirability of an external post-audit.

No university's operations can be poured through the mold of a central state purchasing office with much success. The university should be encouraged to use the services of the state purchasing office in instances where real economies are thus obtainable, where the volume is sufficient to justify it, and where some delay can be tolerated.

If decisions in university administration are all to be siphoned off to the statehouse, then we shall have no further need for institutional governing boards except for ceremonial purposes, and presidents and deans can become civil service clerks. What sort of university would we have then? I leave the answer to you.

The Climate Becomes More Favorable

At least a few enlightened chief state fiscal officers have openly recognized that too much meddling with university administration is not good, and have frequently restrained their subordinates. There seems to be oncoming a sense of decent tolerance and balance between campus and capitol that may relieve the strain that has grown up for decades in many states. This is good news for veteran presidents and business officers who have argued their case for many years, often with virtually no perceptible results.

Looking at the statewide picture, no one doubts that the high-level decisions as to what portion of the state's income shall be invested in higher education and what portions in other state government functions belong to the people through their governor and legislature. State fiscal offices can help by showing the large outlines of the statewide fiscal situation at any given time, but their job is not to manage the institutions, much less to interfere in their management so as unwittingly to impair their efficiency.

The principal universities in Michigan, Minnesota, California and several other states are fortunate in the respect that their state constitutions give the university governing boards full control, and protect them from outside meddling in their internal affairs by non-educational administrative functionaries. First established in Michigan a century ago, this principle is slowly gaining ground.

A state university undoubtedly has a duty to be candid and communicative, but not servile, in its relations with state authorities and the public.

A Landmark and a Redirection

The trend was firmly signalled by the appearance in 1959 of the two reports of the Committee on Government and Higher Education headed by Milton Eisenhower, president of Johns Hopkins University. Composed of some fifteen nationally eminent citizens, the Committee included industrialists, financiers, journalists, and persons in public service, as well as prominent educators, among whom were two veteran state university presidents: Virgil M. Hancher of the State University of Iowa and J. Lewis Morrill of the University of Minnesota.

The succinct report of the Committee itself, in fewer than fifty pages, forthrightly recommends the withdrawal of detrimentally detailed fiscal controls from the statehouse to the state universities and colleges.[1] This, of course, is in harmony with the best current administrative theory applicable in business organizations and in government. It explicitly recognizes, too, that public education, on account of the inherent nature of its processes, has an even stronger claim for a degree of institutional autonomy.

The staff report, documenting the conclusions of the Committee, is a full-scale volume of thirteen fact-packed and fluently-written chapters.[2] The two reports together form a cogent *Magna Carta* for state-supported higher education.

---

[1] Committee on Government and Higher Education. *The Efficiency of Freedom.* Baltimore: The Johns Hopkins Press, 1959. Pp. 44. $1.
[2] Moos, Malcolm, and Francis E. Rourke. *The Campus and the State.* Baltimore: The Johns Hopkins Press, 1959. Pp. 414. $6.

(45)

Coordination of Statewide Systems

The self-control, flexibility, and elbow-room of state universities and colleges are also endangered in varying degrees by well-meant but ill-adapted schemes and plans for the consolidation or coordination of their control on a statewide basis. No one questions that the service of the state's people as a whole should be a first consideration in institutional planning; and that in states having several state-supported universities and colleges, amicable teamwork among them to serve the state's needs in a reasonably cooperative manner is an essential. But teamwork does not wholly preclude some competition; and teamwork should not mean the destruction of opportunity for initiative, experimentation, and originality.

The earliest, simplest, harshest, most abrupt, and probably least satisfactory expedient is the abolition of the governing boards of all state-supported colleges and universities in a state, and the erection in their place of a single *consolidated* structure of control under *one* governing board for the entire state. Between 1896 and 1948 this expedient was adopted by thirteen states in succession. No such step has been taken in any state since 1948, and the movement is perhaps permanently stopped in its tracks. With the exception of New York, the thirteen states are in the West and South, and most of them are relatively small in population and resources.

The newer fashion which has been espoused in nine states since 1941, is that of leaving the several institutional governing boards at least nominally undisturbed, while superimposing a *single statewide coordinating* board which will not be responsible for operating any institution, but which will have specified powers, coercive or persuasive or both, to effect modifications of the programs and budgets of the institutions.

The Oklahoma Regents for Higher Education (1941) by virtue of a provision of the state constitution receive all state appropriations for higher education and allocate the funds among eighteen state-supported institutions. No other statewide *coordinating* board in any other state has this plenitude of power. In general in the other eight states having coordinating boards the authority of such a board is largely limited to analyzing the budgets and programs of the several colleges and universities and making recommendations to the legislature regarding appropriations.

There is unmistakably a strong trend away from compulsion and toward permissiveness and persuasive leadership in the relations between the newer coordinating boards and the institutions within their jurisdiction. In fact, in Wisconsin (1955) and Utah (1959) the very structure of the coordinating agency, as well as its name ("Committee" and "Council" respectively) indicates that it is intended to be an organ of *lateral liaison* as much as a superimposed organ of coordination. In Virginia (1956), Illinois (1957), and North Carolina (as amended 1959), the agency has scarcely more than advisory powers.

Voluntary Coordination

It is important to observe that a third type of expedient, perhaps the best-adapted of all, consists of wholly *voluntary* coordination of the several institutions, through organizations of their presidents, principal staff members, and representatives of their governing boards. This involves no formal statutory bureaucracy at all. One of the leading examples is the Liaison Committee of the Regents of the University of California and the State Board of Education, which has operated for fifteen years and has had much influence upon the orderly development of the largest state system of higher education in the United States, without reducing it to the dead-level of a vast bureaucratic monolith.

Somewhat similar voluntary organizations have been functioning with considerable success for years in Colorado, Indiana, Ohio (Inter-University Council of Ohio), and Michigan (Michigan Council of State College Presidents). There is, indeed, a good deal of activity of this type going on continually even in states which have one consolidated governing board or a superimposed statutory coordinating board. A great deal of it goes on, too, unpublicized and unsung, in numerous states where there is less of formal compulsory coordination of any kind. Currently (in 1960) stirrings in Minnesota, Missouri, Arkansas, Tennessee, South Carolina, and Washington indicate that *voluntary* coordination may be developing to assure reasonable autonomy for institutions and flexible viability for state systems.

(47)

VII

Who Is the University?

The university does not exist for its faculty, nor even for its students, alone. It is a servant of society, and each of its individual agents, of whatever class or level, is in a sense a servant of the public. Therefore the university is appropriately governed, in the eyes of the law, by a body of men and women chosen as representatives of the general public. This body—the governing board, constituting a single artificial person—legally is the university.

The university is an aggregation of students. It is a faculty. It is a president and a substantial number of administrative staff members of various ranks. It is a governing board made up of leading citizens. It is thousands of alumni and former students, scattered throughout the world. It is fathers and mothers of students, nearly all of whom make important financial sacrifices to assure their sons and daughters an education. It is farmers, housewives, small-business men, local schoolteachers, and workingmen who use its experiment-station bulletins, its extension classes, and its publications. It is the private donors, legislators, and taxpayers who contribute to its support. It is the industrial corporations which contract with its faculty members and advanced graduate students for research in its laboratories or which provide fellowships for the same purpose. Increasingly, it is an arm of the national government, with research projects contracted for by such agencies as the Atomic Energy Commission and the Department of Defense, or supported in part by the Public Health Service or the National Science Foundation or the Office of Education.

This chapter was first published under the same title in the *Journal of Higher Education* 30: 320-324 (June 1959).

All these are the university. The picture is inspiring, but it is diffuse. Who really *is* the university? It is reported that a university president, when reminded in conversation that the faculty works for the university, snorted and replied, "The faculty *is* the university." If the story is authentic, this remark may have been made in all sincerity or it may have been made for effect. In a loose sense, it has something to commend it; but if we are to speak with pinpoint precision, it is not the answer. The faculty members are employees of the university. Each has a contract of employment to do certain work for a stipulated period of time and for a specified salary. Who is the other party to the contract? The governing board, called board of trustees, board of regents, board of governors, or some similar name. This body is almost always a corporation—an artificial person having a legal identity quite distinct and separate from that of any of its members or of any other natural person. In the eyes of the law, this ghostly legal entity *is* the university.

The concept is useful, practical, realistic, and necessary. Not only the faculty members, but also the students and the governmental and private sponsors of research, have contracts with the university. Each student at whatever level, whether he knows it or not, has his contract of enrollment, with some of its terms printed in the institutional catalogue and some ascertainable from other relevant documents. In general, it provides that, having accepted him as a student in a given course of study, the university is obligated to afford him fair opportunity to complete the requirements in that course and receive the appropriate certificate, diploma, or degree, unless he himself breaches the contract by failure to maintain the required standards of scholarship or of conduct.

In addition to its contracts with students and faculty members, the university makes thousands of contracts with administrative and other non-academic employees, with suppliers of myriad types of commodities which such an institution must use in its day-to-day operations, with building contractors and landowners, as well as with research contractors and purchasers of surplus products which it has for sale. Essential as it is that there be a legal entity capable of contracting, nevertheless the business operation of the university is distinctly secondary to its selection and pursuit of educational goals. This educational policy-making and -execution is what the university exists for, and this is why it was long ago aptly designated the "developmental arm of society."

To perform this top-ranking function, the people establish a university governing board which is their direct representative. If the board of trustees of a private university is self-perpetuating or co-optive, it is yet in theory a representative of and for the constituency of the institution. Whether the institution is public or private, legally the board *is* the university, not merely for business functioning, but for accomplishing the central and paramount task. The governing board is at the apex of a large community of selected agents. The newest Freshman is an agent of the board, because he has been admitted to the university community and given a job to do. The president is an agent of the board, because he has been appointed the chief executive officer responsible for the operation of the university. Likewise, every member of the faculty, every student, and every non-academic employee is an agent of the board.

The board is composed of a few citizens, laymen in the sense that they are not educators. As individuals, none of them has an iota of legal authority over the university or any of its parts. Collectively, when assembled in duly convened sessions, they have plenary power to manage the university extending to the outward boundaries of the domain of authority established for them in the constitution and statutes of the state, as construed by the courts. There is also a kind of "common law of universities" embracing certain matters which have been the custom of universities for centuries, and which may be invoked by the courts when not specifically negated by statutory law.

These large responsibilities the board discharges mainly through agents of its own choosing; for it could not possibly exercise them directly if it were in session daily; and actually it is usually in session only a day or two at intervals of a month or more. On occasion it may use a committee of its own members as agent for a particular task such as conducting a search for a new president of the university or overseeing a program of investment of endowment funds; but in general the president of the university is its sole and single ranking agent, superior to all others, and alone responsible to the board. He recommends all other employees for appointment, and proposes all changes in the policies and program of the university. The famed Charles W. Eliot of Harvard wisely characterized the board as chiefly an "inspecting and consenting" body. This does not mean that the board is a rubber stamp for the president. It means that the board keeps generally informed about the operation of the university and its standing in the

(51)

state and nation, and in the light of that knowledge approves or dis-
approves proposed new policies.

Organization and Orderly Devolution

Actually, the president delegates much of his authority to administrative officers and faculty, and some to student organizations. This is
customary and necessary; but it must be kept in mind that delegations
of power are revocable, and that devolution of a function does not
remove it from the jurisdiction of the president and the governing
board. It makes no change at all in the locus of the final legal authority
in case of an appeal from an administrative, faculty, or student-organi-
zation decision. The channel of appeal is upward to the president, thence
to the governing board. This is equally true, of course, if the appeal is
from action of a "community government" organization composed of
representatives of students, faculty, and administrative staff. The orderly
progression of appeals must be maintained. Organization disintegrates
if "everybody decides everything."

The practical and operative apportionment of authority among
president, administrative staff, faculty, and students derives from several
sources. The highest of these is the charter of the institution, which, for
example, often says in effect that the governing board may confer
degrees, but only upon the recommendation of the faculty. This gives
the faculty a power which even the governing board cannot derogate.
But beyond this the charters are usually silent, and any other powers
possessed by the faculty come from other sources. In many institutions
the president and faculty have drawn up a constitution for faculty
government which has been formally accepted and approved by the
governing board and published as an ordinance or set of regulations of
the board.

The constitution often provides for a faculty senate and other appropriate organs for the expression of faculty opinion and the formulation
of faculty policies and their transmission to the president and the board.
If approved, new policies thus presented become accretions or amendments to the existing regulations. But any such proposed policy may be
ignored or disapproved by the board, in which event it is of no legal
effect. This provision has occasionally given rise to some pain and
protest on the part of faculty members who take seriously the propo-
sition that the faculty *is* the university, or at least ought to govern the
university. Such is not the plan of university control in this country, as
almost everyone knows; and there are ample reasons for believing that

ultimate legal control by the faculty as a so-called guild of scholars might not be in the public interest.

Writing of his observations of the actual operation of the system as it is, a wise commentator has said, "Between the formal and the informal organization are found many incompatibilities, imponderables, and shams."[1] The statement is true; but some of these unhappy and unresolved features would evaporate if more of the persons concerned at all levels could bring themselves to understand the law and comprehend the relevant principles of administration.

The Spheres of the Students and of the Faculty

The same principles apply to constitutions for student government and for "campus community government." The governing board of the university may accept and approve, through the hands of the president, and publish, as a regulation under the board's authority, a code providing for a student senate, a student council, a student judicial court, or similar organs of student government. This code may, as it sometimes does, stipulate that disputed acts or decisions of student-government agencies shall be appealable to a community-government agency jointly composed of students, faculty members, and administrative officers. Thence the channel of appeal is upward to the president, and finally to the governing board of the university. Any officer in the channel of appeal may reverse, annul, or stay any action or decision appealed from. In other words, student-government actions are, in the last analysis, only recommendations to the legal authority governing the university. In a legal sense, the students are not the university, nor are they self-governing.

Of course, this is not say that student-government organizations or faculty agencies are not effective. In fact, they perform indispensable roles, and generally perform them well. The majority of their actions and decisions stand without protest or appeal to higher authority. Very probably they accomplish much in the maintenance of faculty morale and in the informal education of students in the manner and methods of representative government. A deplorable feature is the prevalence of misconceptions regarding the nature and scope of their authority which engender much needless heat when one of their recommendations is ignored, one of their actions rescinded, or one of their decisions reversed by university agencies possessing legal authority to do so.

[1] Logan Wilson, *The Academic Man* (New York: Oxford University Press, 1942), p. 221.

Students compose one of the "estates" in a university—numerically the largest, unless alumni and parents be counted as "estates." Faculty members comprise another, much smaller in numbers but superior in age, experience, and intellectual discipline. Ideally, however, the differences between students and faculty are merely relative—for all are really students, as becomes most obvious in seminars and colloquia in which faculty members and advanced graduate students participate alike.

A California judge recently pondered this subject when he placed college-owned housing for faculty members in the same tax-exempt category as student residence halls. Said he: "A college with students but no faculty is much more of an anomaly than one with a faculty but no students. In our conception of the term, a faculty and student body, for all practical considerations, are necessarily co-existent if there is to be a college."[2] It is not to be overlooked that faculty members stand *in loco parentis* to their students who are under the age of majority; that their relation to all their students is a fiduciary one, in many respects comparable to that of physician and patient, or lawyer and client; and that faculty members have the non-delegable, quasi-judicial duty of adjudging fairly the quality of the academic work of their students. Moreover, councils and committees of the faculty perform an enormous amount of essential work in formulating and modifying the various curriculums and maintaining the requirements for admission and graduation.

For purposes of affording channels for the free expression of opinion, for the formulation of consensuses, as well as for the disposition of a considerable amount of administrative detail which must necessarily be delegated to them, student governments and faculty governments are all to the good; but the idea of vesting actual legal authority at a high level in "guilds" or "estates" is a medieval relic of feudal times. The university does not exist for its faculty, nor even for its students, alone. It is a servant of society, and each of its individual agents, of whatever class or level, is in a sense a servant of the public. Therefore, the university is appropriately governed, in the eyes of the law, by a body of men and women chosen as representatives of the general public. This body—the governing board, constituting a single artificial person—legally *is* the university. Complete understanding of this simple concept could go far toward clarifying the roles of subordinate organizations, all of which have their useful spheres in the intricate complex of university administration.

---

[2] *Church Divinity School of the Pacific v. Alameda County*, 152 C. A. 2d 496 (1957).

VIII

Where Will the Money Come From?

Stepping up the tax support of tuition-free higher education is the simple, practicable, equitable way of keeping opportunity open and of making the most of America's intellectual resources.

By 1970, college and university enrollments will be doubled, and the cost of operating the institutions is likely to be tripled. Operating costs will increase from roughly $4 billion a year at present to $10 billion or more in 1970. Where will the additional $6 billion a year come from?

State governments are now appropriating about $1.5 billion a year for higher education, almost all of it for state-supported institutions. The federal government's contribution to operating funds, except through contracts and grants for organized research, is as yet comparatively small. In 1959, it amounted to about $500 million.

Students are paying about $1 billion. Most of this goes to private institutions, in which, on the average, student fees supply 55 to 60 per cent of the operating costs; in public institutions, they amount to an average of about 20 per cent. Private gifts are being received at a rate of about $1 billion a year. Income from invested funds and miscellaneous other sources provides smaller amounts.

Thus the three major suppliers at the present time are the state governments, students who pay fees, and private benefactors. Frankly, among the other smaller sources, only one—the federal government—seems capable of making a substantially larger contribution than at

This chapter was first published under the same title in the *Journal of Higher Education* 31: 257-262 (May 1960). It is an adaptation of a paper presented at the annual meeting of the Education Section of the American Association for the Advancement of Science in Chicago, December 29, 1959.

present. Private gifts are increasing at a moderate rate. They come from alumni, church organizations, business corporations, philanthropic foundations, citizens of surrounding communities, and other friends of the institutions. They are encouraged by federal and state tax laws, and will continue to increase.

Many private institutions are raising student fees, but the public universities and colleges are reluctant to do so, remembering that they were intended in practically every instance to be free of tuition charges and, in contrast to the aristocratic tradition, open to able sons and daughters of working people.

If student fees continue at the level they are now, by 1970 the doubling of enrollments will produce an additional $1 billion a year. Private gifts will probably yield another $1 billion annually within a decade. We face a momentous decision. Shall the additional $4 billion come from tax funds, or shall this burden be shifted to the students and their families? Shall education be a public service, or a commodity for those able to pay for it?

A century ago we decided once and for all that public education is an essential public function, and that schools and colleges will be maintained at public expense. Do we want to revive the ancient argument about the alleged injustice of compelling the bachelor to pay taxes to support the schools for his neighbor's twelve children? More than a century and a half ago, both the federal government and the states began to endow public schools and universities with public lands. Is this splendid policy now to be abandoned? Certainly we should make no such reversal when the development of all available talents in the public interest seems more imperative than ever before.

Traditionally we allow private colleges and universities to manage their own affairs—academic as well as fiscal. If they think it necessary to raise their fees, they can do so and continue to fulfill a useful purpose by educating those able to pay. But if their fees approach or reach a level sufficient to pay the full costs of operation, they break faith with the generations of private donors who have contributed to their endowment funds in order to provide education at less than cost. It is true that a few of the great private universities can be highly selective, if they choose, on a basis of financial ability as well as intellectual capacity in their choice of students. But even they can price themselves out of the market. Perhaps that is why some of their representatives appear so desperate in their efforts to induce other private colleges, as well as state institutions, to raise student fees inordinately. The fact is that 60 per cent of all college and university students are now in public institutions; by 1970, probably 80 per cent will be there. This shifting of the balance will be no calamity. From any standpoint, it will be preferable to having large numbers of able students denied the opportunity to attend college because they cannot afford to pay excessive fees.

Some say that a system of scholarships can solve all of our problems. Actually, a majority of all scholarships available are worth less than the cost of tuition, and it is not uncommon for an assistantship to pay $500 for $1,000 worth of work. Adequate scholarships would involve the vast sums that can come in these days only from the national government. To administer such a scheme, a vast bureaucracy, even if decentralized, would be inevitable; and it would bring with it invasions of privacy which no one wants. It is much simpler to keep the campus gates open to all able students by keeping the public colleges and universities tuition-free or available at a merely nominal cost. This is the only way to make sure that all able students will have their chance and that all available talent will be developed.

Many Reasons Condemn the Policy of Raising Student Fees in Public Institutions

From some quarters it is urged that student fees should be doubled in public institutions and raised to cover nearly full costs in private institutions so that perhaps an additional $3 billion a year would be taken from students by 1970. Coupled with this is the preposterous proposal of a scheme of long-term private borrowing in which families would pay for education as they now pay for ranch-type housing and hard goods. Those who advocate long-term loans to pay for higher education ignore the fact that few students are willing to mortgage their future; that no girl wants to saddle a prospective husband with a long-term debt; that this scheme discriminates grossly against women when more than ever we need educated woman power; that all state universities and colleges were originally intended to be the capstones of *free* public school systems.

It is often loosely stated that a college graduate stands to gain $100,000 or more in lifetime earnings because of his college attendance. Obviously this is not true of all graduates, especially of women; and even if it were true, how can it justify requiring the student to pay for his education at a time when he is young, untrained, and unable to do so? If he later earns an additional $100,000, he will pay more than the cost of his educa-

(57)

tion in income taxes on that extra income. Moreover, in later life, he is quite likely to make gifts to his own college or to other schools. All this he can do with less hardship than high tuition fees would have caused in his youth.

Besides squeezing out many capable students who cannot pay, and thus losing to the nation the opportunity of developing their talents, the shortsighted high-fee policy produces other deplorable consequences. By falling more harshly upon women than on men, it helps to cut off the supply of sorely needed educated persons in such professions as nursing, teaching, and social work. Worst of all is its unquestioned tendency to cause many students to focus their ambitions on high-paying jobs so that they can get out of college and make a "fast buck" and pay off their college debts. This motivation is not conducive to the best use of the college years, and hardly creates an atmosphere favorable to an impartial search for truth. The worst damage that a high-fee policy can do to a college or university is to degrade its students' aims and encourage mercenary motives.

Education Is Not a Purchasable Commodity

Fortunately, a high-fee policy for public universities will not be necessary. The $4 billion a year which will be needed by 1970 can be supplied from governmental sources. The whole could come from the federal government if as little as 5 per cent of current federal budgets were allocated to the states for this purpose.

Four billion dollars now represents about 1 per cent of the gross national product. If, by 1970, the gross national product rises to $600 billion, as most economists think it will, then an expenditure of $10 billion a year for higher education would be about 1.7 per cent. If the increase frightens anyone, he need only observe that the Soviet Union is now said to be expending about 3 per cent of its gross national product annually for higher education.

It is not likely that the United States will continue indefinitely to spend tens of billions a year for the maintenance of hundreds of military bases in all parts of the world. In fact, the development of new weapons has already practically destroyed the usefulness of many of these bases. But the annual expenditure of $40 billion by the federal government for defense is a powerful stimulus to business. Will a reduction cause an economic collapse? Certainly not, if we redeploy a part of the funds thus released to the support of higher education in this country. And this investment will yield future as well as immediate gains.

To preserve the freedom and diversity of American higher education, we need to let each state control its own system. If this is to be done, we must stop making federal appropriations only for narrowly specified educational purposes such as agricultural extension, vocational training, medical education, and so on, and begin giving grants without special conditions to the states for the broad purpose of developing their own systems of higher education.

The states can more than double their support of higher education by 1970. Reports received from forty-five states show that for the current fiscal year (1960) $1.5 billion was appropriated for the operating expenses of higher education, which is an increase of more than 20 per cent over comparable appropriations of two years earlier.[1] If this rate of increase is merely maintained for a decade, the fifty states will be appropriating at least $3 billion by the fifth biennium.

Superficially, one may get an impression that some states are nearly insolvent. This is an erroneous notion. Although state revenues and expenditures have increased greatly in the last fifty years, it is not at all difficult to observe that the modernization of state tax systems has taken place rather slowly. Of course there are wide differences in the resources of the states; but we have a solid core of populous industrialized states, with enormous, rapidly increasing wealth, whose state taxes per capita are comparatively low.

Significantly, forty-five years ago the states were devoting an average of 10 per cent of their total annual expenditures to the support of higher education; this year, on the average, they are spending only 4 to 6 per cent of the total for higher education. Obviously, we do not esteem higher education as highly as we did. Here again, there is wide variation among the states, partly because some states rely heavily upon private colleges and universities, whereas some have no institutions of this type. Nevertheless, the states are spending comparatively less for higher education than they did in 1915.

Tremendous increases have occurred especially for highways and welfare activities, stimulated by federal matching grants. This has resulted in some distortion of the appropriate balance among state

---

[1] These figures were first reported on pages 71 and 72 of the October, 1959, issue of "Grapevine," a mimeographed newsletter privately circulated by the author.

expenditures, now overdue to be redressed. However, many states made progress in 1959 toward modernizing their revenue systems.

The idea of lowering state taxes to get new industries into a state is rapidly being supplanted by the realization that enlightened corporate management is attracted by good public-school systems and especially by the research facilities and research leadership found in well-supported state universities. Competition among the states to provide the best of these facilities is much more in the public interest than the older race to cut down essential public services in order to offer outsiders the inducement of low taxes or no taxes.

Higher Education Is a Public Function

The history of 1959 shows that the states are aware of their responsibility for higher education and are meeting it increasingly well. Seven of the forty-five states replying to queries report a two-year increase of 33 per cent or more in their appropriations. These are Alabama, Alaska, Arizona, Hawaii, Nevada, New Mexico, and Rhode Island. Only three states—Arkansas, South Carolina, and South Dakota—show an increase of less than 10 per cent. Increases of 17 to 25 per cent were made by many of the more populous states which have the greatest influence on the national picture. Among these are California, Illinois, Indiana, Iowa, Louisiana, Michigan, Missouri, New Jersey, New York, North Carolina, Ohio, and Oklahoma.

To note increases in appropriations of state tax funds does not, of course, afford a comprehensive picture of the financing of higher education. Several of the larger state universities are currently deriving over half of their annual operating expenses from sources other than state appropriations—from student fees, private benefactions, contract payments and grants for research from the federal government, and grants from private industries and philanthropic foundations.

But certainly we need to know where we are going in the area of state appropriations, and how fast we are moving. A two-year or a four-year period is, of course, too short a time to provide a basis on which to make sweeping conclusions. For example, some of the states making small increases for the current fiscal period may have made very large increases four years ago or six years ago. These matters can be ascertained by anyone who wishes to examine the biennial reports of the U.S. Office of Education on higher educational finances. However, these reports are not generally available until a couple of years after the particular biennium has elapsed. I was able to report the state appropriations of 1959 before the year ended only because of the kindness of my correspondents in the state capitals.[2]

The extremely wide range of percentages of biennial increases in appropriations is from 1.5 per cent to more than 100 per cent. Neither of the extreme rates will be maintained indefinitely; but the width of the range suggests some interesting possibilities. Continuation of these observations over a period of several bienniums will be a fascinating study.

Progress Goes On

Clearly, it is possible, short of some unforeseen economic disaster, for the fifty states to make rapid progress toward greater support of higher education. Some states will be able to do much better than others. Fortunately, many of the abler states are among the largest and most populous. In planning for rapidly expanded financing of higher education, we must not sell the states short. They are now furnishing more support than any other major source, and their contribution is increasing rapidly. Additional support from the federal government will not mean any slackening of state support.

Currently, the bulk of federal support is in the form of large-scale financing of research undertakings, to which the states have not yet contributed in much volume or with much enthusiasm. In the future, if federal support assumes a more generalized form, as we hope it eventually will, it can easily be predicated upon full maintenance or a reasonable increase of the state's contribution. If by 1970 the state appropriations are two and a half times what they are now, and the federal support amounts to four times what it is today, we shall be able to lift the burden of fees from students in public colleges and universities and forget the nightmare of a vast bureaucratic system of scholarships which would take money out of one pocket and put it into another. An uncompromising "meritocracy" could really be a horror! Stepping up the tax support of tuition-free higher education is the simple, practicable, equitable way of keeping opportunity open and of making the most of America's intellectual resources.

Progress is being made, despite frequent setbacks and temporary defeats. The record of accomplishments in the state legislative sessions in

---

[2] M. M. Chambers, "State Appropriations for Higher Education, 1959," *College and University Business*, XXVII (November, 1959). pp. 81-83.

any recent year is not without encouraging features, and every year has a few high points that are positively thrilling. Communication grows better. Public concern about higher education becomes more intense and more informed. State support grows larger in volume and more conducive to institutional freedom to develop in the public interest. Greatly augmented federal support to the states is accepted as indispensable and inevitable. A better-balanced partnership of the three levels of government, adjusted to conditions in each state, can be attained. The states will continue to be the parents and guardians of most public institutions of higher education, and their legislatures will continue to be a primary source of growing appropriations of public money.

IX

Something Can Be Done
About State Revenues

*Not all the states have done all that is possible to de-
velop diversified, equitable and productive tax systems. In
fact, economic and technological progress make it repeatedly necessary for the states to revise and modernize their
revenue systems. This process is going on.*

With creeping inflation and leaping growth of population, every state
needs more money for public education. Each commonwealth contributes from state-collected funds at least some portion of the operating
costs of local school units; in fact, the average for all the states is now
above 40 per cent. Other essential public services, including higher
education, highways, health and welfare, to mention only a few, also
require state support. Where is the money coming from?

Have the states exhausted their sources of revenue? Have they done
all that is possible to develop diversified, equitable and productive tax
systems, and to keep them up to date? Happily, the answer is *No*. Evidence is supplied by what happened in more than forty state legislatures
in 1959 and 1960. New revenue measures were reported from nearly a
score of state capitals where legislatures had acted before mid-August
of 1959.

Sales Taxes Raised and Extended

Arizona stepped up the general sales tax from 2 cents on the dollar to
3 cents, and will use two-thirds of the revenue to increase state aid to
local schools. *Washington* raised the general sales tax rate from 3⅓

This chapter was first published under the same title in the *American School
Board Journal* 139 (No. 4): 31-32 (October 1959).

cents on the dollar to 4 cents. Other productive tax revisions are expected to produce $112 million of new revenue during the biennium. *Pennsylvania* increased the general sales tax rate to 4 cents on the dollar.

Michigan enacted a 'use tax' of 1 cent on the dollar, to be added to the existing 3-cent general sales tax, making the practical equivalent of a 4-cent sales tax rate. The additional cent would have produced $120 million a year of new revenue. This measure was soon invalidated, however, by a decision of the state supreme court holding it in violation of a constitutional prohibition of a sales tax rate above 3 cents. Accordingly a proposed amendment to the constitution, to permit the higher rate, was put on the ballot for the general election of 1960.

South Carolina extended the coverage of the current 3 per cent general sales tax to include retail electricity, telephone, telegraph, laundry and dry-cleaning charges. This state also placed a 10 per cent tax on sales of admission tickets to amusement events other than high school and church entertainments and sports. *Ohio* altered the scale of purchases to which the general sales tax applies, so as to bring in an estimated $33½ million added revenue during the next biennium.

Utah authorized the counties to levy optional countywide general sales taxes of one-half of 1 per cent, for support of county and municipal governments.

General sales taxes are hugely and promptly productive. They are regressive (tending to bear heavily upon the lower income classes) but this feature is to some extent countervailed by exempting some of the staple necessities of life, and largely counterbalanced by having a progressively graduated income tax as a part of the same revenue system.

The big news of the legislative year 1960 came early in the year, when *Kentucky* became the thirty-fourth state to enact a general sales tax. The new measure establishes a rate of 3 cents on the dollar. About one-third of the proceeds will be used to pay a state soldiers' bonus, and approximately two-thirds will go for public education, financing much-needed increases in salaries for teachers in elementary and secondary schools, and enabling substantial budget expansions to be made for the state institutions of higher education.

Income Taxes Undergoing Improvement

The idea of placing state income tax collections on a withholding basis, after the manner of the federal income tax, is gaining ground rapidly. In *Massachusetts* the withholding system went into effect February 18, 1959, and is expected to increase the revenue by $50 million. *New York* state's collections by withholding began April 1. *South Carolina* also enacted a withholding plan. *Utah's* income tax withholding, hitherto applicable only to nonresidents, is extended to cover residents as well. *North Carolina* and *Oklahoma* also enacted new withholding systems.

The state individual income tax law in *New York* was extensively revised so as to bring in an estimated $112 million of new revenue this year. Personal exemptions, formerly $1,000 for a single person, $2,500 for a married couple, and $400 for each dependent, are reduced to a uniform $600 per person. New brackets at the upper end of the scale of rates raise the top bracket to 10 per cent on taxable income above $15,000. Formerly the top was 7 per cent on income above $9,000.

The *New York* legislature approved, subject to popular referendum, a constitutional amendment which would allow the legislature to conform state income tax requirements to the federal without specifying in detail each such change. A recess study of questions involved in conforming state to federal tax law practices was directed, and $200,000 appropriated to finance it. This is a significant matter, for it may lead to methods whereby the states can collect their income taxes at a minimum of administrative expense.

California revised the personal income tax law to produce an additional $60 million this year and $71½ million next year. The brackets increasing the rate by 1 per cent each now span $2,500 intervals instead of $5,000 as before, and the maximum rate is raised from 6 per cent to 7 per cent, applicable to incomes above $15,000 instead of the former $25,000.

Oregon revised the income tax law to produce an additional $12 million biennially, chiefly by eliminating the allowance of the amount of federal income tax paid as a deduction from taxable income under the state law. Also, a taxpayer choosing to pay his income tax in quarterly payments instead of a whole year at once, will have to pay interest at the rate of 1 per cent per month on the deferred installments. This is expected to bring in an additional $6 million. The new act also embraces a state capital-gains tax.

South Carolina eliminated the former exemption of up to $500 for federal income taxes paid; and added two new brackets at the upper range of the scale to catch higher incomes. *Idaho* changed the income tax structure to include increased rates, elimination of an income tax credit of $5 for each dependent, adoption of the federal exemption structure, and addition of a $10 surtax on each income tax return filed. *Iowa* raised the corporate income tax rate from 2 per cent to 3 per cent.

In *Minnesota* the corporate income tax rate was stepped up from 7.3 per cent to 9.3 per cent. Rates on individual incomes were raised by one-half of one per cent. The tax credit for dependents was changed from $10 to $14.

A dozen states as yet have no income tax law. Three states have neither an income tax nor a general sales tax. These two taxes together form the core of a productive and equitable modern state revenue system.

Other Sources of Revenue Available

New York revised the inheritance tax schedules to produce an estimated $10 million a year in new revenue. In *Oregon* a revamped inheritance tax law will bring in more than $3 million additional for the biennium. *Minnesota* increased the inheritance tax rates somewhat.

The special sales taxes, such as those on motor fuels, alcoholic beverages, cigarettes and other tobacco products, and gambling tickets, are substantial sources of income. State gasoline taxes are raised in *New York* from 4 cents to 6 cents per gallon (diesel fuel 6 cents to 9 cents); from 6 cents to 7 cents in *West Virginia;* and from 5 cents to 7 cents in *Ohio* and *Vermont.* The boost of 2 cents in *Ohio* is expected to produce $120 million a year additional revenue.

Texas enacted for the first time a number of special sales taxes on luxury items, mostly at 3 per cent of the selling price. Items covered include furs and precious stones; cosmetics, perfumes and beautifiers; hotel and motel room rentals; air conditioners; and boats and motors. Existing special sales taxes on radio and television sets, motor vehicles, wines and liquors, and all tobacco products except snuff, were substantially raised.

New York City's sales tax of 3 cents to the dollar on restaurant meals is raised to 5 cents, effective June 1, and will bring in $13 million. An additional $100 million for the city will come from six other new or increased taxes: the 2-cent rise in the cigarette tax (from 1 cent to 3 cents a pack); an increase in the gross receipts tax for general business (up from one-fourth of one per cent to two-fifths of one per cent); a raise of 1 per cent (up from 1 per cent to 2 per cent) on the gross receipts tax for utilities, and a raise of the gross receipts tax on financial businesses (up from 1 per cent to 1½ per cent); a new tax of one-half of 1 per cent on sales of real estate above $25,000; and an impost of $25 a year on jukeboxes.

Vermont levied a tax of 3 per cent on lodging in hotel rooms and purchase of meals.

Washington raised the base tax on liquors from 10 per cent to 15 per cent; increased the tax on cigarettes from 5 cents a pack to 6 cents; levied a 25 per cent tax on tobacco products other than cigarettes. In *Idaho* cigarette taxes were stepped up from 4 cents a pack to 5 cents; in *Wyoming*, from 3 cents to 4 cents; in *Iowa*, from 3 cents to 4 cents; in *Minnesota*, from 4 cents to 5½ cents. *Ohio* also enacted a 2-cent raise.

Minnesota also boosted the tax on other tobacco products from 15 per cent to 20 per cent on the wholesale price, and increased the taxes on beer and liquors.

Raising the prices of state-sold liquors is another source. New statutes on this subject in *Ohio* will bring an additional $20 million a year in net profits. *Oregon* will gain $3 million by the same method.

New York increased the number of days for thoroughbred and harness racing to get $5 million additional yearly revenue from the tax on the sale of pari-mutuel tickets. *Ohio* raised the tax on horse-race wagering, to produce an additional $7 million.

West Virginia raised the motor vehicle license fees, and levied a highway tax on trucks. *Utah* doubled the oil and gas severance tax, boosting it from 1 per cent to 2 per cent. *Minnesota* increased the severance tax on iron ore from 13.65 per cent of the adjusted net value at the mouth of the mine to 14.25 per cent. *Texas* added a 1.5 per cent tax on the value of gas bought by the first purchaser (severance beneficiary), aimed chiefly at the big pipelines.

Business and occupation taxes were stepped up somewhat by *Washington* and *West Virginia*. *New Hampshire* enacted, effective in 1960, a franchise tax on gas and electric companies, to amount to 8 per cent of their net income derived from within the state. *Ohio* adopted a corporation franchise levy which will bring in $60 million of new money during the biennium.

Texas boosted corporation franchise taxes by 22 per cent, with a 33 per cent increase for this year only. *Michigan* raised slightly the business activities tax on general business, while raising the exemption to $12,500 of gross receipts, thus letting out about 10,000 small businesses. The business activities tax on utilities was also raised, and the intangible property tax on bank deposits was stepped up by 10 cents on each $1,000.

The Outlook Becomes Clear

A very favorable straw-in-the-wind is the fact that the worn idea of the states competing with each other to attract new industries by avoiding taxation, especially personal and corporate income taxes, is well on the wane. Instead it is now recognized that enlightened corporations looking for plant sites are strongly drawn by the advantages of good public school systems, as well as by the research facilities and research leadership afforded by the presence of great state universities. Education is the endless frontier.

The path ahead is plain. Consider, for example, seven large and populous states whose legislatures were recently more or less deadlocked on tax measures. Texas and Nebraska had neither an income tax (individual or corporate), nor a general sales tax. Illinois, Michigan, and Ohio had no income taxes. Minnesota and Wisconsin had no general sales taxes. All these great commonwealths face the opportunity of bringing their revenue systems up to date.

X

Higher Education Is
A Public Obligation

We shall have more and better education for more people than ever before, and the high points of excellence will be higher than hitherto. The prospect ought not to be regarded with misgivings, but with confidence and enthusiasm.

Education, including college and university education, is a public responsibility. Although private educational institutions, especially private colleges and universities, are given only the lightest of surveillance by the states and are allowed practically complete autonomy in the management of their fiscal and academic affairs, their existence is at the sufferance of the states, and they are required to meet at least nominal standards maintained by the states. Governments (state and Federal) not only permit them to exist, but also actively encourage and assist them by tax exemptions and numerous other means. All this is on the theory that they perform a *public function* which otherwise would have to be performed at public expense by the use of tax funds.

Our governments do not set out to monopolize the function of education or to make of it a monolithic public service. Instead, they allow private effort to operate as a partner in the same enterprise. Thus, we maintain a pluralistic system, with maximum freedom of choice for founders, teachers, students, parents, and financial benefactors. That this makes for strength and richness and viability scarcely surprises anyone.

Higher education is a public obligation because society as a whole is its principal beneficiary.

This chapter was first published in *School and Society* 88: 283-285 (Summer 1960).

Of course, the duty to develop his own talents to the optimum level sets squarely upon each individual, and to say that education is a public function does not relieve him of that. From him must come the consuming motive; from society should come the provision of the opportunity. For many persons in the earlier years of college this means accessibility within commuting distance of their homes; and for many it means the maintenance of free tuition or low fees. This is why the local public junior college—or community college—is undergoing a tremendous expansion today and why a great many state universities and colleges have kept their fees at modest levels.

The Balance Is Shifting

Partly because of these reasons, about 60 per cent of all college students in the U. S. are now in public institutions and 40 per cent in private ones. The balance is shifting and will continue to shift; but this does not at all imply that private institutions will become any less numerous, or any smaller, or have any fewer students or less financial support than they have today. In fact, the total of private gifts is steadily increasing, and the private colleges may reasonably expect to see their incomes grow, their students become somewhat more numerous, and their physical facilities expand a little. But this will take place at a rather restrained pace; and only to a very minor extent will it cope with what half a decade ago was aptly and widely named "the tidal wave of students" in the 1960's. There are few among the 50 states in which it has not been reliably estimated that the numbers of college students will be doubled by 1970; and in several, such as California, Nevada, Arizona, and Florida, there is good reason to believe they will be tripled.

The bulk of the job will fall on the public institutions—from junior college to graduate school; and the proportion of all students in private colleges may decline from today's 40 per cent to perhaps 20 per cent. This will be no calamity. There will be greater opportunity for the private colleges to be more selective and to continue their role of making the national picture of higher education more diversified than it would be without them. This role always will be important.

The President's Commission on Higher Education in 1947 found that half of the college-age population of the U. S. was intellectually capable of deriving substantial benefit from at least two years of college education and that one-third of the whole college-age group could complete four years of college with success. The younger of the college-age people of 1970 are already enrolled in the second and third grades of the elementary schools. Their total numbers can be estimated with accuracy. Why must we provide two years of college for half of them and four years for a third of them, plus advanced graduate and professional education for unprecedented numbers? Why can we not be more selective and choose only those who have the money to pay high fees, plus those who are in the upper three per cent or five per cent in intellectual capacity as measured by tests?

The People Will Decide

We shall follow no such short-sighted restrictive policies because they primarily are in conflict with deeply felt and widespread aspirarations of nearly all Americans. These questions will not be decided by educators or by politicians, or by bankers or by orthodox economists of 19th-century vintage. The wants of the masses of men and women will decide. No sentiment is more common than "I want my boy to have a better job than I have had," and "I want my girl to have a higher station in life than I have known." Are these yearnings narrowly selfish, unreasonable, and unworthy of attention? Not necessarily. They contain a strong vein of self-renunciation, as witness the financial sacrifices made by millions of parents to keep their children in college—the mothers who do the weekly laundry that comes from college by parcel post and the fathers who deny themselves necessities, to provide money for college expenses.

Is it possible that every reasonably competent boy can expect to have a better job than his father had? Not literally in every case, of course, but, by and large, in almost all cases it is not only possible but probable. The breathtaking advances in technology that follow one another cause an upgrading of all jobs, from highest to lowest. There is less and less need for the unskilled and more and more demand for the skilled worker, the technician, the middle-grade subprofessional or semiprofessional, and on up through the ranks of operating engineers and other professionals to the topmost levels of design engineers and creative scientists in all fields.

These facts need no documentation, but let us compare them with the recently published paper of an assistant secretary of labor in the current, conservative national administration who, looking at the 1960's, said,

"There will be a rise in the level of training and educational requirements of jobs all across the board," and "professional workers will be by far the fastest growing of all the major occupational groups." He went on to say that "Technicians who work with and give technical support to engineers and scientists will also be very much in demand. Employment in these technician occupations has shot upward during the past two decades." Further, "The emphasis on a college education is strong in modern business and government and will probably become stronger in the future, in view of the steadily increasing body of knowledge and skill required for many fields of work." Finally, "To insure that college facilities and staff are expanded as required to meet personnel needs in different fields is a goal of highest priority from the viewpoint both of our national strength and of the life opportunities of millions of young men and women."[1]

There is no question as to whether we shall provide high-quality education for relatively small numbers of the best brains or whether we shall afford appropriate types of education for larger and larger numbers of competent young persons who are not rated in the topmost intellectual strata. We shall do both. We cannot do less if we are to maintain leadership in the Space Age. In 1900, four per cent of the college-age population were attending college. By 1960, the percentage has moved up to well above 30. It will move on up to 40 and 50 before it levels off. Long ago have we left behind us the concept of higher education as a narrow ladder for a stringently selected few, destined only for a handful of "prestige professions," chiefly law, medicine, and theology. Now there are literally scores—even hundreds—of occupations in which some college training is either a prerequisite or a decided advantage. Higher education in America is becoming a vast and varied system, with courses of study varying from a few weeks to eight or ten years in duration and of types and levels suited to different intellectual qualities and aptitudes as well as diverse occupational choices. There are honorable exits at the end of two years, four years, five years, and at intermediate points for those who wish to terminate their formal schooling early.

Since the educated person is a better producer and a better consumer, the increase in productivity and in buying power adds more than enough to the national income to recoup the cost of education.

Eventually, the states and the Federal government will work together as partners, as they already do to some extent, in providing the neces-

---

[1] N. Brown, *Higher Education*, 16: 3-6, Dec., 1959.

sary expansion of facilities for public higher education. The national urgency of the purpose justifies a relative increase in the Federal share, which will be forthcoming. We shall have more and better education for more people than ever before, and the high points of excellence will be higher than hitherto. The prospect ought not to be regarded with misgivings, but with confidence and enthusiasm.

INDEX

Michigan State University, 2, 24
Michigan, University of, 2, 7, 11, 12, 17, 24
Minnesota, 43, 45, 66, 67, 68
Minnesota, University of, 24, 45, 47
Mississippi, 28
Missouri, 47, 60
Montana, 24
Moos, Malcolm, 45 n.
Morrill Act, 23
Morrill, James Lewis, 45

National Science Foundation, 49
Nebraska, 68
Nevada, 60
New Hampshire, 67
New Jersey, 60
New Mexico, 24, 60
New York, 46, 60, 65, 66, 67
North Carolina, 60, 65
North Central Association of Colleges and Secondary Schools, 29-30

Ohio, 25, 47, 60, 66, 67, 68
Ohio State University, 24
Oklahoma, 60, 65
Oklahoma Regents for Higher Education, 46
Old Siwash, 9-16
Oregon, 65, 67

Parents, aspirations of, 71
President's Commission on Higher Education (1947), 6, 70-71
Private colleges, 11, 26, 56, 69, 70
Protestant church-related colleges, 25
Public Health Service, 49
Purchasing, 44

Research, nature and importance of, 9, 14-21

Rhode Island, 60
Roman Catholic colleges, 25
Roman Catholic parochial schools, 31
Rourke, Francis E., 45 n.

Sales taxes, state, 63-64
Scholarships, 57-61
Seltzer, Lawrence H., 3
Stanford University, 11
South Carolina, 47, 60, 64, 65, 66
South Dakota, 60
State support of higher education, 59-61
Student government, 53-54

Tappan, Henry Philip, 11
Tax systems, state, 63-67
Tennessee, 47
Texas, 12, 66, 67, 68
Thaden, John F., 2

United Nations, 19
U. S. Department of Commerce, 31
Utah, 47, 64, 65

Vermont, 66, 67
Virginia, 47
Voluntary coordination, 47

Washington, 12, 47, 63-64, 67
Wayne State University, 2
West Virginia, 66, 67
Wilson, Logan, 53 n.
Wisconsin, 47, 68
Wisconsin, University of, 24
Wyoming, 67

Youth surveys, 33